LANGUA(

Dorothy
Celia Genishi an
ADVISORY BOARD: *Richard A*
Anne Haas Dyson, Carole Edelsky,

MW00465604

Educating for Empathy:
Literacy Learning and Civic Engagement
NICOLE MIRRA

Preparing English Learners for College and Career:
Lessons from Successful High Schools
MARÍA SANTOS ET AL.

Reading the Rainbow: LGBTQ-Inclusive Literacy
Instruction in the Elementary Classroom
CAITLIN L. RYAN & JILL M. HERMANN-WILMARTH

Educating Emergent Bilinguals: Policies, Programs, and
Practices for English Learners, 2nd Edition
OFELIA GARCÍA & JO ANNE KLEIFGEN

Social Justice Literacies in the English Classroom:
Teaching Practice in Action
ASHLEY S. BOYD

Remixing Multiliteracies: Theory and Practice from
New London to New Times
FRANK SERAFINI & ELISABETH GEE, EDS.

Culturally Sustaining Pedagogies:
Teaching and Learning for Justice in a Changing World
DJANGO PARIS & H. SAMY ALIM, EDS.

Choice and Agency in the Writing Workshop:
Developing Engaged Writers, Grades 4–6
FRED L. HAMEL

Assessing Writing, Teaching Writers: Putting the
Analytic Writing Continuum to Work in Your Classroom
MARY ANN SMITH & SHERRY SEALE SWAIN

The Teacher-Writer: Creating Writing Groups
for Personal and Professional Growth
CHRISTINE M. DAWSON

Every Young Child a Reader: Using Marie Clay's
Key Concepts for Classroom Instruction
SHARAN A. GIBSON & BARBARA MOSS

"You Gotta BE the Book": Teaching Engaged and
Reflective Reading with Adolescents, Third Edition
JEFFREY D. WILHELM

Personal Narrative, Revised:
Writing Love and Agency in the High School Classroom
BRONWYN CLARE LAMAY

Inclusive Literacy Teaching: Differentiating Approaches in
Multilingual Elementary Classrooms
LORI HELMAN, CARRIE ROGERS, AMY FREDERICK, & MAGGIE STRUCK

The Vocabulary Book:
Learning and Instruction, Second Edition
MICHAEL F. GRAVES

Reading, Writing, and Talk: Inclusive Teaching Strategies
for Diverse Learners, K–2
MARIANA SOUTO-MANNING & JESSICA MARTELL

Go Be a Writer!: Expanding the Curricular Boundaries of
Literacy Learning with Children
CANDACE R. KUBY & TARA GUTSHALL RUCKER

Partnering with Immigrant Communities:
Action Through Literacy
GERALD CAMPANO, MARÍA PAULA GHISO, & BETHANY J. WELCH

Teaching Outside the Box but Inside the Standards:
Making Room for Dialogue
BOB FECHO, MICHELLE FALTER, & XIAOLI HONG, EDS.

Literacy Leadership in Changing Schools:
10 Keys to Successful Professional Development
SHELLEY B. WEPNER, DIANE W. GÓMEZ, KATIE EGAN CUNNINGHAM,
KRISTIN N. RAINVILLE, & COURTNEY KELLY

Literacy Theory as Practice:
Connecting Theory and Instruction in K–12 Classrooms
LARA J. HANDSFIELD

Literacy and History in Action: Immersive Approaches to
Disciplinary Thinking, Grades 5–12
THOMAS M. MCCANN, REBECCA D'ANGELO, NANCY GALAS,
& MARY GRESKA

Pose, Wobble, Flow:
A Culturally Proactive Approach to Literacy Instruction
ANTERO GARCIA & CINDY O'DONNELL-ALLEN

Newsworthy—Cultivating Critical Thinkers, Readers, and
Writers in Language Arts Classrooms
ED MADISON

Engaging Writers with Multigenre Research Projects:
A Teacher's Guide
NANCY MACK

Teaching Transnational Youth—
Literacy and Education in a Changing World
ALLISON SKERRETT

Uncommonly Good Ideas—
Teaching Writing in the Common Core Era
SANDRA MURPHY & MARY ANN SMITH

The One-on-One Reading and Writing Conference:
Working with Students on Complex Texts
JENNIFER BERNE & SOPHIE C. DEGENER

Critical Encounters in Secondary English:
Teaching Literary Theory to Adolescents, Third Edition
DEBORAH APPLEMAN

Transforming Talk into Text—Argument Writing, Inquiry,
and Discussion, Grades 6–12
THOMAS M. MCCANN

Reading and Representing Across the Content Areas:
A Classroom Guide
AMY ALEXANDRA WILSON & KATHRYN J. CHAVEZ

Writing and Teaching to Change the World:
Connecting with Our Most Vulnerable Students
STEPHANIE JONES, ED.

Educating Literacy Teachers Online:
Tools, Techniques, and Transformations
LANE W. CLARKE & SUSAN WATTS-TAFFEE

Other People's English: Code-Meshing,
Code-Switching, and African American Literacy
VERSHAWN ASHANTI YOUNG, RUSTY BARRETT,
Y'SHANDA YOUNG-RIVERA, & KIM BRIAN LOVEJOY

WHAM! Teaching with Graphic Novels Across
the Curriculum
WILLIAM G. BROZO, GARY MOORMAN, & CARLA K. MEYER

continued

For volumes in the NCRLL Collection (edited by JoBeth Allen and Donna E. Alvermann) and the Practitioners Bookshelf Series
(edited by Celia Genishi and Donna E. Alvermann), as well as other titles in this series, please visit www.tcpress.com.

"Treat Others the Way You Want to "Be Treated""

Educating *centers the self ≠ empathy*

for Empathy

LITERACY LEARNING
AND CIVIC ENGAGEMENT

Nicole Mirra

Foreword by Ernest Morrell

from German: "Einfühlung" meaning "to feel into" Born in 1909!!!

TEACHERS COLLEGE PRESS
TEACHERS COLLEGE | COLUMBIA UNIVERSITY
NEW YORK AND LONDON

1234 Amsterdam Avenue
New York, NY 10027-6602

NATIONAL WRITING PROJECT

2105 Bancroft Way
Berkeley, CA 94720-1042

Published simultaneously by Teachers College Press, 1234 Amsterdam Avenue, New York, NY 10027 and National Writing Project, 2105 Bancroft Way, Berkeley, CA 94720-1042.

Through its mission, the National Writing Project (NWP) focuses the knowledge, expertise, and leadership of our nation's educators on sustained efforts to help youth become successful writers and learners. NWP works in partnership with local writing project sites, located on nearly 200 university and college campuses, to provide high-quality professional development in schools, universities, libraries, museums, and after-school programs. NWP envisions a future where every person is an accomplished writer, engaged learner, and active participant in a digital, interconnected world.

Cover design by adam b. bohannon.

Material in Chapter 1, Chapter 4, and Conclusion from the DML Blog "From Connected Learning to Connected Teaching: A Step Forward and "What Do We Mean When We talk About 21st Century Learning" are used with permission of the University of California Humanities Research Institute.

Library of Congress Cataloging-in-Publication Data is available at loc.gov

Names: Mirra, Nicole, author.
Title: Educating for empathy : literacy learning and civic engagement / Nicole Mirra ; foreword by Ernest Morell.
Description: New York, NY : Teachers College Press, [2018] | Series: Language and literacy series | Includes bibliographical references and index.
Identifiers: LCCN 2018017419| ISBN 9780807759141 (pbk. : alk. paper) ISBN 9780807777282 (ebook)
Subjects: LCSH: Language arts (Secondary)—Social aspects. | Literature—Study and teaching (Secondary)—Social aspects. | Empathy—Study and teaching (Secondary) | Civics—Study and teaching (Secondary)
Classification: LCC LB1631 .M457 2018 | DDC 428.0071/2—dc23
LC record available at https://lccn.loc.gov/2018017419

ISBN 978-0-8077-5914-1 (paper)
ISBN 978-0-8077-7728-2 (ebook)

Printed on acid-free paper
Manufactured in the United States of America

25 24 23 22 21 20 19 18   8 7 6 5 4 3 2 1

Contents

Foreword

Frankfurt School theorist Theodor Adorno begins his 1966 essay "Education After Auschwitz" with the now famous lines, "the premier demand of all education is that Auschwitz not happen again. Its priority before any other requirement is such that I believe I need not and should not justify it . . . never again Auschwitz." Adorno taps into two truths that critical educators have held onto for most of the past century: (1) that the education children receive can increase hatred and barbarism in the world, and (2) that a critical and reflexive educational experience can help increase the authentic dialogue, intercultural understanding, and civic action that may help significantly reduce acts of hatred and intolerance in our increasingly heterogeneous and interconnected society.

Unfortunately, like Adorno, we must continually justify a critical approach to teaching and learning. The global industrial rhetoric around primary, secondary, and tertiary education prioritizes workplace readiness, quantifiable literacy, and numeracy skills above all else. It is rare to find any measure of school system success that includes kindness, empathy, or a proclivity to act toward justice in the world. As Marian Wright Edelman, president and founder of the Children's Defense Fund would say, "Shame on us!" Although academic literacy rates are rising domestically and internationally, and more young people than ever are accessing secondary and tertiary education, we see daily—in acts of violence, prejudice, intolerance, and oppression—the need to revisit Adorno's question: What good is increased access to education if it does not serve to make the world a more peaceful and connected community?

Professor Mirra is a key contributor of a growing community of contemporary scholars who are addressing this question in provocative and, I argue, transformational ways. An unfortunate (and grossly inaccurate) dichotomy persists in our current educational discourse between a desire for a rigorous, objective scientific education that produces relevant and quantifiable 21st-century skills and a fear of a "theoretical" and ideological education that, though possibly well intentioned, produces irrelevant feel-good outcomes at best and antipatriotic activists with few economically beneficial skills at worst.

I mention Mirra's work as transformational. During the decade that I have known and followed her work closely, she has always been interested in a both/and approach that brings some synthesis to this troubling, yet persistent dichotomy. That is, how can education increase civic dialogue while also fostering academic and critical literacies for our most vulnerable populations? It is in this hybrid third space that *Educating for Empathy: Literacy Learning and Civic Engagement* positions itself.

Like Adorno, Mirra begins by addressing the empathy deficit in schools and society. Toward this end, she asks what kinds of educational practices can reverse the empathy deficit and produce compassionate, democratically engaged young adults. Mirra further argues that, "the development of empathy in students (and teachers) should be considered a primary goal of education because it offers an organizing principle for our field that is grounded in hope, love, and a commitment to a more equitable society" (citation from Mirra introduction).

Mirra's book is distinctive in many ways but its most important contribution is that she takes up these questions in the very specific context of English education. How can English teachers, in their daily interactions with students, address disciplinary content while also fostering empathy and civic engagement? How can we conceptualize literacy to encompass active citizenship and a regard for others? How can English teachers utilize the imaginative texts of our discipline like novels, plays, poems, memoirs, films, musical lyrics, and digital narratives to foster what Maxine Greene calls a *social imagination* in the service of what Mirra terms a *critical civic empathy*?

Mirra's critical civic empathy allows space for students to make the moves we want them to in English classes as they study literary texts seriously in that it encourages them to analyze positions of power and privilege. However, she also offers a vision for how we might push the field of English education into civic relevance by drawing upon these powerful novels, poems, and plays to foster dialogue and even civic action. What might high school students want to do differently in the world after reading and discussing Toni Morrison's *Beloved*?

The beauty of this book is that Mirra takes us into English classrooms across the country to show us what teachers and students actually *do* with texts like *Beloved* to develop critical civic empathy. Whether it is an English classroom in South Los Angeles, a debate program in Brooklyn, a Youth Participatory Action Research project, or a National Writing Project network, the book is eminently pragmatic in its everyday examples of curricular and pedagogical innovation. It is also inspirational and aspirational for a discipline that is continually considering how to reinvent English so that it remains provocative, responsive, and sustaining to present and future generations of teachers and students as we struggle daily to bring, in Mirra's words, more joy and justice to classrooms and to civic life.

—Ernest Morrell,
South Bend, Indiana
May 12, 2018

Introduction

How do you think you would react if a member of your immediate family told you they were going to marry someone of a different race? How about a gun owner? Or someone who does not believe in God?

Imagine you are moving to another community. Would living in a place where most people share your political views be important to you?

Think about elected officials in Washington who share your positions on the most important issues facing the nation. Should they work with elected officials they disagree with, even if it results in some policies you don't like?

Several years ago, the Pew Research Center (2014) posed these questions in a survey to a nationally representative sample of 10,000 U.S. adults. The primary purpose of the survey was to explore political polarization; however, considering the extent to which these questions grapple with our interactions with people who hold different perspectives and experiences from our own, it also can be seen as a sort of referendum on empathy. These questions, in effect, were asking: Can you work with, live with—even love— people unlike yourself?

The responses suggested that empathy was in dangerously short supply, and follow-up data from the Pew Research Center (2017) indicate that the trends are continuing to worsen. Many citizens are retreating into ideological silos in which their political views determine not only how they vote, but also whom they befriend, where they live, and how they define political progress. Media experts warn that too many of us are learning about and responding to these challenges from news outlets and social networks that reflect our existing opinions and biases back to us, creating what they call an "echo chamber" effect (DiFonzo, 2008). Facebook algorithms seek to determine our political persuasions and direct us to like-minded content, while cable news networks predictably interpret (and sometimes bend or obfuscate) facts to appeal to liberal or conservative voters. The overall message that emerged from the study: We hold fiercely to our views, we want to be surrounded by others who share them, and we don't want to compromise with those who don't.

Thus, we find ourselves in a scenario in which civic life is becoming more divisive and rancorous as the United States faces serious 21st-century challenges that require cooperation and compassion. Consider the issues making headlines today—divisions of race, class, religion, and legal status are roiling communities across the country as we argue over whose lives matter, who belongs in our country, and what it means to be American. #BlackLivesMatter. Undocumented student DREAMers. Debates over Muslim bans.

If you are thinking to yourself that this kind of divisiveness does not reflect your beliefs or experiences, you are not alone. The great majority of Americans have much more nuanced perspectives and diverse sets of loved ones than this portrait portrays; however, the urgent problem exposed by the Pew study is that folks on the far ends of the ideological spectrum have become the most active participants in nearly every aspect of the political process and increasingly are commanding the tone and tenor of the country's public discourse. They are speaking in the town square with megaphones while the rest of us whisper among ourselves.

This phenomenon is not new. Back in 2006, before he became president, then-senator Barack Obama named this problem and warned of the consequences of a lack of empathy in our civic life in a commencement speech at Northwestern University. It is a warning that in hindsight seems like an ominous preview of the political divisiveness that loomed over his administration and has been leveraged in that of his successor.

In the speech, Obama (2006) lamented a political culture that encouraged "selfish impulses" and the tendency of people to "live in neighborhoods with people who are exactly like yourself, and send your kids to the same schools, and narrow your concerns to what's going on in your own little circle." He named the consequences of such a narrowing of concerns: "They will tell you that Americans who sleep in the streets and beg for food got there because they're all lazy or weak of spirit. That the inner-city children who are trapped in dilapidated schools can't learn and won't learn and so we should just give up on them entirely."

He then declared:

> There's a lot of talk in this country about the federal deficit. But I think we should talk more about our empathy deficit—the ability to put ourselves in someone's shoes; to see the world through those that are different from us—the child who's hungry, the laid-off steelworker, the immigrant woman cleaning your dorm room.

Empathy. The concept is now popping up with regularity in news articles and opinion pieces—it seems as if everyone is thinking about who should be empathizing with whom and how all of us can be empathizing more, particularly in the wake of the polarizing 2016 U.S. presidential election.

While all Americans should be concerned about a diminished public life and the state of empathy in society, why should educators in particular be attuned to this situation? The short answer is: because we will be expected to do something to address it. Public schools have been called upon again and again by our country's political leaders to rectify social ills, from poverty to drug abuse to lagging economic competitiveness (Tyack & Cuban, 1995), and the newest call involves combating ideological isolation. And the race to figure out how to teach empathy is on—*Education Week* recently published a piece titled "Building Empathy in Schools," while the website Edutopia has offered think pieces including "Empathy: The Most Important Back-to-School Supply" and "Empathy in the Classroom: Why Should I Care?"

I will build upon this question with some of my own. What role (if any) should schools play in fostering empathy in students? What, for that matter, *is* empathy? And what kinds of educational practices can reverse the empathy deficit and produce compassionate, democratically engaged young adults?

I suggest in this book that the development of empathy in students (and teachers) should be considered a primary goal of education because it offers an organizing principle for our field grounded in hope, love, and a commitment to a more equitable society. Embracing a purpose to shape young adults who can step outside their personal experience to compassionately imagine the lives of others and act civically based upon those experiences can help our profession prioritize and streamline our practice so that, instead of feeling pulled in a million different directions, we stand committed to one. We can create lessons, implement routines, and develop relationships with students in ways that are empowering instead of overwhelming. It is easy to focus on the daily pressures of lesson planning when faced with changing content standards and high-stakes tests, but unless we remind ourselves of the ultimate outcomes that we want our instruction to achieve for our students, we become lost in the weeds and forget the greater purpose of public education. We forget why we teach in the first place.

So, let's explore this concept and its connection to schools in more depth, particularly as it relates to English education.

WHAT IS EMPATHY? WHY IS IT IMPORTANT?

The most commonly understood definition of *empathy* is the one that Obama (2006) used in his speech—the ability to put yourself "into another person's shoes" or see the world from that person's perspective. Empathy often is confused with sympathy, compassion, and pity, although it differs in subtle but crucial ways. The German translation of "feeling into" helps differentiate empathy from these other terms because it speaks to the idea of moving beyond oneself and *into* the perspective of another person. Psychologists associate empathy with "theory of mind," or the ability to analyze the world from a frame of reference completely separate from one's own— this often is referred to as "cognitive empathy." It can be compared with "emotional empathy," or the phenomenon of being affected by someone's emotional state and then feeling or responding with a similar emotion.

Empathy is considered a crucial part of emotional intelligence because of the hypothesized causal relationship between cognition and action. If we are able to adopt the perspectives of those unlike ourselves, then perhaps we are more likely to make decisions and take steps that benefit not only our own selfish interests, but the interests of those other people as well. Writ large, empathy becomes the foundation for a democratic society—the way to keep a heterogeneous citizenry working together without descending into mob rule. And as with many of our democracy's most important character traits, we look to schools to help instill them in our students.

EMPATHY AND ENGLISH EDUCATION: OPPORTUNITIES AND BARRIERS

Even if not named explicitly, empathy has long had a place in U.S. public schools, most often through the idea that schools should produce individuals of good character who will be responsible democratic citizens. Indeed, empathy is crucial for democratic governance, considering the need for individuals from diverse backgrounds to accept beliefs that are not necessarily their own. While I will argue in a moment that schools often take a reductive view of good citizenship (simply being a kind person rather than participating in civic life), along with a reductive view of empathy through a focus on niceness (think of the golden rule) rather than true perspective-taking, these concepts certainly rank in the constellation of traits that parents and community leaders expect schools to promote (Phi Delta Kappan, 2016).

Furthermore, because many authors and social psychologists connect the development of empathy to storytelling, curriculum developers and teachers often turn to English classes in particular as cultivators of compassion (Zunshine, 2006). Consider this quote from author and social critic James Baldwin (Howard, 1963):

> You think your pain and your heartbreak are unprecedented in the history of the world, but then you read. It was books that taught me that the things that tormented me most were the very things that connected me with all the people who were alive, or who had ever been alive. (pg. 89)

Building upon Baldwin's assertion that literacy (and literature) possess unique power to connect all people, I consider literacy education a crucial focal point for the development of empathy. English teachers occupy a uniquely powerful position when it comes to educating for empathy because they are charged with shaping literate individuals—an awesome responsibility that encompasses not merely teaching the skills of reading, writing, listening, and speaking, but also mentoring students to use these skills to carve out personal, professional, and civic identities; grapple with the enduring joys and sorrows of what it means to be human; and contribute to the continuing conversation about how we should best live together in this interconnected society. As a result, I argue that English teachers have a responsibility to help students navigate relationships with others and think about empathy.

Furthermore, English teachers have the opportunity to use imaginative texts (e.g., novels, poems, films, memoirs, creative nonfiction, digital stories, etc.) as catalysts for learning, which can provide a springboard to the development of empathy. Philosopher Maxine Greene (2000) argues that reading allows young people to develop a "social imagination" that they can use to imagine various selves and different visions of a just society. Once students can imagine a range of possible worlds, they are better prepared to begin building the ones they want to see.

Yet we must acknowledge the systemic barriers that stand in the way of fostering empathy in the English (or really any other) classroom within today's educational landscape. The first roadblock is one that is felt powerfully by many teachers today: namely, a focus on standardized testing and a high-stakes accountability system that serves to narrow how literacy is taught. In an exhaustive review of 11 recent adolescent literacy reports, a group of researchers found that education policy promotes a definition of literacy focused solely on academic reading skills that prepare students for college and career readiness, offering little space for students to "think critically about the world they inhabit and develop their own alternative literacies" (Faggella-Luby, Ware, & Cappozoli, 2009, p. 470). As a result, many teachers feel that they do not have the time to grapple with the civic elements of literacy or integrate considerations of empathy into their practice.

Furthermore, state standards and professional resources consistently minimize the role of English language arts as a discipline that engages with democratic life by situating social studies as the primary home of civic education. And, increasingly, civics classes focus on general character education rather than the knowledge, skills, and dispositions needed to engage in today's contentious political arena. Civics standards are often vague, overly reliant on factual knowledge, and impossible to achieve in the given time frames (Gagnon, 2003). In addition, civic education curricula often utilize patriotic, triumphalist rhetoric that ignores student experiences and does "not connect to [students'] . . . own identities as citizens" (Torney-Purta & Vermeer, 2004, p. 14).

As a result, much of what passes for civic education today embodies a depoliticized vision of citizenship that education researchers Joel Westheimer and Joseph Kahne (2004) dub the "personally responsible" model. This model operates from the assumption that "to solve civic problems, citizens must have good character; they must be honest, responsible, and law-abiding members of the community" (p. 240). The problem that Westheimer and Kahne identify with this model is that none of these good character traits is *necessarily* connected to a democratic system of government and civic life; as they explain, many dictators would be happy if their citizens embodied these traits. Without more attention to what it means to participate in the structures of power of our democratic system, let alone to analyze the flaws in these structures, civic education falls far short of preparing students to tackle the political challenges of our time.

And I argue that this depoliticization is also happening with understandings of empathy. Much of how empathy is conceptualized in popular culture and in schools involves each of us as individuals seeking to understand the experiences and perspectives of other individuals, with the goal of creating a nicer, more understanding society. While this personal perspective on empathy is valuable, I fear that it risks minimizing or downplaying a broader systemic understanding of the social forces that shape our personal experiences. We are individuals, but our individuality is couched within overlapping social constructs, including race, class, gender, and sexual orientation, that have historical, economic, and political ramifications. If we as individuals seek to empathize with others as individuals, we are likely to, first, interpret experiences in ways that revert to what is familiar to us and, second, miss out on the significance of those social constructs for how we interact in public life.

These consequences are problematic because we are living in a democracy suffering from deep inequities in almost every facet of public life. Researchers have provided exhaustive documentation of the discriminatory treatment that minoritized populations continue to experience in public systems of criminal justice (Alexander, 2010), health (Centers for Disease Control and Prevention, 2013), housing (Desmond, 2016), and education (Lipman, 2011). And these inequities extend into civic life as well. In our society, it is increasingly those on the privileged side of entrenched inequities of race and class who speak in a powerful monologue to elected officials in order to promote and protect their interests (Bartels, 2008). As the American Political Science Association Task Force (2004) noted, "Citizens with lower or moderate incomes speak with a whisper that is lost on the ears of inattentive government officials, while the advantaged roar with a clarity and consistency that policy-makers readily hear and routinely follow" (p. 1).

In fact, we must consider that the very ideas of empathy and perspective-taking are politicized and inequitable. Those with more power across any number of social constructs, from race and gender to religious and sexual orientation, often fail to consider their perspectives as just that—*perspectives*—because they are so accustomed to seeing them represented as the norm in society. By contrast, those with less power constantly are forced to navigate the views of others in order to survive, while seeing theirs minimized, othered, or outright ignored. Calling for students to learn empathy without taking these power dynamics into account can easily become an exercise in papering over generations of implicitly and explicitly enforced hegemony.

Despite (and indeed, because of) these challenges, I suggest that we English educators should prioritize the development of empathy in students as an overarching goal for our field—but a new vision of empathy that is explicitly committed to grappling with the inequities in our public life and engagement with democratic power structures. I propose a new concept to guide our work—critical civic empathy.

MOVING TOWARD A THEORY AND PRACTICE OF CRITICAL CIVIC EMPATHY

Critical civic empathy is about more than simply understanding or tolerating individuals with whom we disagree on a personal level; it is about imaginatively embodying the lives of our fellow citizens while keeping in mind the social forces that differentiate our experiences as we make decisions about our shared public future. Critical civic empathy has three defining principles:

1. It begins from an analysis of the social position, power, and privilege of all parties involved.
2. It focuses on the ways that personal experiences matter in the context of public life.
3. It fosters democratic dialogue and civic action committed to equity and justice.

Let's quickly break down the ways that the adjectives *critical* and *civic* modify *empathy* in crucial ways.

Highlighting the "Critical" Aspect of Empathy

As mentioned above, a personal perspective on empathy downplays the fact that we as individuals belong to a range of overlapping social groups and that these social groups vary in the amount of power they have in society. Taking a critical perspective on empathy encourages us to interrogate what we each bring to the table when we seek to empathize with others and to acknowledge the fact that the ways in which we are privileged (or marginalized) in public life inevitably influence how we interpret the experiences of others.

The idea of destabilizing our assumptions and questioning what appears normal to us originates with a group of German intellectuals in the 1940s who united under the banner of critical theory to push back against the idea of objectivity in research. Philosophers Max Horkheimer and Theodor Adorno (1947) contended that what often is assumed to be common sense in society in fact represents the experiences of those with social power, while the experiences of those who are marginalized are downplayed or outright ignored. Critical theorists highlight the need to expose what is taken for granted in order to dismantle dominant ideas that perpetuate inequality.

This critical tradition has transformed understandings of literacy. In *Literacy: Reading the Word and the World*, Paulo Freire and Donaldo Macedo (1987) define the purposes of reading and writing according to this critical perspective; they argue that in order for literacy to be meaningful, "it has to be situated within a theory of cultural production and viewed as an integral part of the way in which people produce, transform, and reproduce meaning" (p. 142). They explain that literacy must be judged according to whether it serves to "reproduce existing social formations" or to "promote democratic and emancipatory change" (p. 141).

Theorists of critical literacy stress that texts do not exist in a vacuum but are "situated" products of the world that transmit cultural and political messages; in turn, the act of reading these texts must be viewed as a simultaneous reading of the world (Barton, Hamilton, & Ivanic, 2000; Gutierrez, 2008). They argue that literacy can be a force either for cultural reproduction, in which dominant discourses are reinscribed onto the readers as passive objects, or for cultural production, in which the readers become active subjects combing the texts for connections to their daily lives and experiences in order to forge individual and collective self-determination (McLaren & Kincheloe, 2007; Morrell, 2008).

Thus, a critical perspective on empathy in the literacy classroom stresses the idea that we are not all simply individuals devoid of context who come to the task of understanding one another on a level playing field; instead, we are individuals who constantly are negotiating our positions in society and need to deconstruct what we take for granted in order to truly seek to "feel into" someone else's experience. While it is a much more complicated proposition than simply telling students to be nice or to imagine how someone else feels, engaging in critical civic empathy is possible and, when taken seriously, allows for the kind of connections that are needed to break through the forces of divisiveness and polarization that structure our civic life.

Highlighting the "Civic" Aspect of Empathy

Empathizing with someone on a personal level is certainly a worthy endeavor; indeed, it is often through making connections with individuals unlike ourselves that we begin to develop a social consciousness. Yet it is only through couching the personal in the public and understanding the ways in which our personal experiences shape (and are shaped by) our participation in civic life that we can make empathy a more powerful driver of engagement and action for equity and justice. The ultimate goal of critical literacy is not simply to comprehend texts—it is to use the power of text for social transformation; as a result, critical literacy is linked to our civic identities.

Civic identity refers to one's understanding of and relation to a particular community, as well as one's sense of agency to act within it (Youniss, McLellan, & Yates, 1997). Many theorists of civic identity build upon Erik Erikson's (1968) work in adolescent identity development, in which he argues that adolescence is the period in which young people attempt to figure out where they fit within the social structures of their particular communities and countries by engaging with different available ideological options for what society should look like.

Educational philosophers Robert Lawy and Gert Biesta (2007) argue that citizenship is a practice rather than a possession and that young people enact their civic identities through their "participation in the actual practices that make up their daily lives" (p. 45). Psychologists Roderick Watts and Constance Flanagan (2007) highlight the fact that adolescents' daily lives take place within a complex and often unequal social context; as a result, they promote a model of civic (what they call sociopolitical) identity development that centers on a critical rather than normative understanding of the systemic forces shaping society. This model is important to my approach to critical civic empathy because it acknowledges and validates the various ways that young people experience life in the United States and offers them multiple avenues for developing liberating political efficacy rather than a single narrative.

Considering the overlapping social influences on students' civic identities, educators play a huge role in mediating discourses about democracy and influencing how students think about themselves as civic agents. I argue that situating critical civic empathy as a guiding principle for literacy education can help English educators connect their subject matter to the world outside the school doors and position their students not simply as children, but as developing citizens of a democracy badly in need of their energy and leadership.

Distinguishing Critical Civic Empathy from Other Dispositions

As I mentioned earlier, *empathy* has become a popular buzzword in education in the wake of increasing polarization in U.S. society. It can be difficult to parse exactly how the term is being defined when it emerges in the rhetoric of pop culture or professional development. What exactly separates the concept of *critical civic empathy* from other uses of the term *empathy*? In order to provide some clarity, I have created a typology that identifies the key concepts at play in how we think about various understandings of empathy (see Figure I.1). This typology seeks to act as a tool to guide thinking rather than a full encapsulation of society.

The horizontal axis of the typology refers to the concept of mutual humanization, or the idea that we cannot fully realize our own humanity unless and until we recognize and honor the full humanity of those who differ from us. I argue that any serious consideration of empathy must engage with the idea that my existence is wrapped up in yours, as your freedom is wrapped up in mine. This idea is grounded in Paulo Freire's (1970) discussion of learning as a process of conscientization in which teachers and students must engage together in reflection and action aimed at breaking down structures of oppression that ensnare us all.

Mutual humanization intersects with the vertical axis of the typology, which is an orientation toward social and political action. This axis asks us to consider the extent to which empathy goes beyond the golden rule and engages in the messy arena of the political sphere in pursuit of equity and justice. While action is inherently wrapped up in humanization (and vice versa), I tease the concepts apart here for the purpose of highlighting both as necessary precursors to a vision of empathy that truly takes into account and challenges systemic inequities.

These two axes can help us evaluate expressions related to empathy in public life. First, we must acknowledge that there are many examples of speech and action that embody the exact opposite of empathy—examples of individuals striving to foster fear of others and sow seeds of division and political cynicism. I label these as expressions of *imaginative refusal* because they show no concern for mutual humanization and seek to break down rather than build up faith in collaborative democratic action to address the challenges we face as a nation. They represent individuals who lack the imagination needed to relate to others or the will to develop it.

But there are also those who, while they have no true interest in mutual humanization, utilize the rhetoric of empathy for craven political gain. Within this category, which I call *false empathy*, I place politicians who talk about the virtues of "American values" or the "American people," but in a coded way that refers to only *some* values or *some* Americans with whom they agree. The language of empathy can be dangerous when it is applied selectively—when only certain people who share your race or political beliefs or cultural background are viewed as the "we" who deserve compassion and the favor of government resources. The axes of the typology encourage us to read expressions of empathy critically and be wary of those who speak of social harmony but advocate policies of social division and tribalism.

The third category in the typology—*individual empathy*—refers to the aforementioned most popular understanding of empathy as the ability to walk a mile in someone's shoes while avoiding consideration of what it means to support them as a fellow citizen. Again, if we claim to empathize

Figure I.1. Typology of Empathy

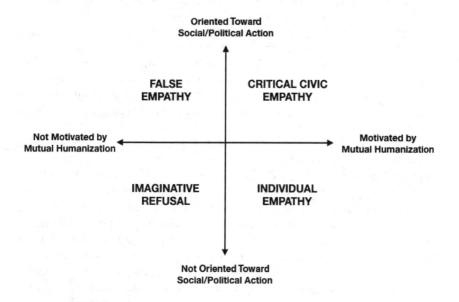

with someone who differs from us in any of the social constructs that stratify public life but then do not vote in favor of policies that would help redress past injustices or prevent future injustices, our compassion remains at the individual level and can serve to maintain an inequitable status quo. An interest in mutual humanization is desirable, but it is the link to social action that brings empathy to fruition as a uniquely democratic disposition.

I want to linger for a moment on the concept of individual empathy because I believe that many current efforts to integrate empathy into schools take this perspective. By illuminating its motivations, I hope to expose its inability to foster the mutual humanization and social action needed to achieve justice and equity—and demonstrate the need for a critical civic vision of empathy instead. I use the proliferation of social–emotional learning programs as a case study of individual empathy.

Critiquing the Social–Emotional Learning Perspective on Empathy

Social–emotional learning (SEL) has a somewhat nebulous definition and is largely a catch-all term referring to the range of skills and competencies that are not directly academic, but are helpful for success in school, that we want to instill in young people. These include kindness, honesty, responsibility, and trustworthiness—in essence, the "soft skills" of being a good human, student, and citizen. The Collaborative for Academic, Social, and Emotional Learning (CASEL), a research and advocacy group at the forefront of promoting SEL, created an infographic highlighting its five main focus areas, one of which is to help students "feel and show empathy for others."

In theory, CASEL advocates for an expansive approach to schoolwide SEL: freestanding SEL lessons, the adoption of project-based learning frameworks, and the integration of SEL into disciplinary instruction. In practice, however, the great majority of SEL curricular resources simply involve explicit instruction about character traits; for example, when it comes to empathy, CASEL's website suggests that "children can be taught through modeling and coaching to recognize how they feel or how someone else may be feeling."

While some studies suggest that such explicit lessons may be effective (Durlak, Weissberg, Dymnicki, Taylor, & Schellinger, 2011), and though I have no inherent objections to discussions of character, I find the SEL approach to empathy problematic in two ways that speak to the larger issues with individual empathy itself. First, making SEL instruction a freestanding project distinct from content instruction creates a qualitative distinction in which character development is considered a separate endeavor from academic learning; that is, learning what it means to be a good human and citizen is one thing, while learning English language arts is something else entirely. This divide gives the impression that academic learning is politically and civically neutral, which is not the case. This lets subject areas off the hook from the responsibility of taking a cold, hard look at the messages being sent about society through academic content instruction. And as long as a high-stakes accountability culture remains in place in public schools, academic learning will always take priority, with SEL lessons a secondary and disposable concern.

My second, and much deeper, concern is that the SEL model conceptualizes empathy at the individual level and puts this disposition to work not in fostering cross-cultural understanding and equity-oriented social change, but in maintaining obedience to the social and educational status quo. The SEL model promotes individual empathy without recognition of the social constructs that influence our individual lives and the power and privilege that accompany those social constructs; as such, it has no goals beyond fostering niceness and certainly no aspirations to building a more responsive civic sphere.

Indeed, CASEL's website specifically indicates that the main goal of SEL is improved academic achievement. The growing research base mentioned earlier that is aiming to quantify the benefits of SEL defines these benefits in terms of test scores and grades. This means that in addition to narrowly envisioning empathy at the individual level, SEL proponents are enlisting it, along with other character traits such as self-awareness and perseverance, to encourage students to succeed in the school system (and, by extension, society) as it is. The underlying belief here is that students need to change or improve themselves in order to meet the needs of schools and society, which are generally sound and not in need of reform.

This belief minimizes the aforementioned systemic inequities within U.S. society and promotes the personally responsible vision of citizenship. To tell young people that they will have equal opportunities to succeed if they play by the rules and treat others as they would like to be treated harms all young people. For those on the privileged side of inequities, this rhetoric can blind them to the structural forces working in their favor and leave them thinking that individual merit alone causes their successes; for those on the marginalized side, it can leave them with deficit orientations about themselves or their communities and cause civic alienation. The idea that constructs like race and class will cease to structure the experiences and opportunities of individuals and communities if we simply ignore them and focus on our common humanity is not only misguided, but dangerous, for it both allows the stratification to continue *and* attempts to silence the dialogue that is the first step in doing something about it.

This is why I advocate for a model of critical civic empathy that is grounded in recognition of these constructs and uses them as the starting point for transformative social dialogue and action. Only through this recognition can dialogue truly honor the experiences of young people across the spectrum of U.S. life and create the foundation for a clear-eyed, shared future characterized by collective rather than personal visions of success. In the chapters to come, I tell the stories of teachers and students striving toward critical civic empathy within the messiness of real classrooms and real life.

PUTTING CRITICAL CIVIC EMPATHY INTO PRACTICE

Each day, students come to class brimming with questions and concerns about the events going on in the world beyond the school building. They want to know more about what is happening in their communities and the world at large. They want to know what these events mean for their futures. They want to know what their teachers think about these events. And each day, teachers struggle to explain a complex, often troubling world to their students while also balancing the demands of imparting content knowledge and academic skills.

Parents and teachers want schooling to do more for children than simply prepare them for college and careers. They put their trust in education to produce future generations that will be ready to tackle the challenges to come with thoughtfulness, grace, and compassion. Often, they just aren't sure how to do it—and critical civic empathy offers an entry point into this work.

Implementing a pedagogy of critical civic empathy in the English classroom requires teachers to analyze the role that politics plays in our practice. This involves exploring who we are, who our students are, and how multiple and often contradictory ideas and experiences interact with one another during the learning process. Most important, it involves considering the implications that our literacy practices have for participation in civic life outside of school.

These considerations can lead us to reimagine some of the most foundational practices of our discipline. For instance, the study of literary texts in class can be conceptualized as not simply an exercise in analyzing figurative language, author intent, and theme, but also an opportunity to expose students to life experiences that reflect and/or differ from their own. Classroom debates can be seen as not simply structured academic discussions, but also opportunities to consider multiple perspectives and develop counterarguments aimed at fostering authentic civic deliberation. Research papers can become opportunities for students to take on roles as knowledge producers rather than mere knowledge seekers, and digital expression can become a means of real-world communication across boundaries of time, space, and geography. I will explore each of these practices in the chapters to come.

ORIENTATION AND STRUCTURE OF THE BOOK

I have designed this book to offer an accessible and engaging synthesis of theory, research, and practice so that teachers and teacher educators will be inspired to think about the purposes of literacy instruction, learn about the innovative literacy practices other educators have developed, and then design transformative literacy opportunities that promote empathy and civic engagement in their own contexts.

Because this book is drawn from my experiences working with students and teachers, I find it necessary to add a small note about the orientation toward this work that I bring to the table. I began my career as a high school English teacher and debate coach in Brooklyn, New York—a middle-class, White, cis-gender, heterosexual woman teaching low-income Black and Latinx youth. Before I started teaching, I did not interrogate the power and privilege from which I benefited as result of my identities, largely because I had internalized many of my experiences and perspectives as normal and unremarkable. My trajectory hewed nicely to the dominant U.S. narrative of success and progress, and it took entering the classroom for me to begin the process of reflection in which I now engage continuously in order to deconstruct my assumptions and strive to become a socially conscious and justice-oriented educator.

My students have always been (and continue to be) my guide in this journey. My early years of teaching shaped my commitment to critical literacy and civic engagement, particularly for young people whose voices often are minimized or ignored in the political process and in public life in general. As I learned about my students' experiences outside of the classroom, I began to realize that it was more important to me that they learn how to use their literacy skills to advocate for themselves and their communities than that they remember, for instance, all of the lines of Hamlet's "To Be or Not to Be" soliloquy (although these goals need not be mutually exclusive and certainly were not in my classroom).

Though the practices I consider in these chapters are relevant to students and teachers across contexts, I explore them largely in the context of working with students from communities most marginalized in civic life in cities ranging from New York to Los Angeles. And this is precisely because I see amplification and support of these students' voices as a crucial step toward making American civic life more equitable and just. Also, I would like to note that while pseudonyms are used throughout the book for student, school, and some teacher names, several of the educators whose work I discuss wanted their true names used to share pride in their work and support for mine. Thanks to Jerica, Ashley, and Ben for entrusting me with your stories.

To this end, Chapter 1 draws upon my study of two high school English teachers in South and East Los Angeles to examine the ways that reading and interpreting literature can help students develop critical civic empathy. I focus on the ways that creative texts offer imaginative access into the lives and minds of others in ways that can inspire students' civic identity development. I share teachers' practices as they introduce texts to their classroom and facilitate discussions with their students, highlighting student and teacher voices. The chapter concludes with thoughts about how teachers can choose texts that highlight particular social issues.

In Chapter 2, I share my past experiences as a high school debate coach and my current work studying how debate is being integrated into middle schools in New York City in order to analyze the impact of debate on the development of students' critical thinking, collaboration, and critical civic empathy skills. I offer an in-depth portrait of a middle school in Brooklyn that demonstrates how debate encourages students to consider multiple perspectives on controversial social issues as they establish their own beliefs. I explore how debates that begin in the classroom can extend into community spaces as students participate in weekend tournaments that bring them into contact with peers and adults from across the city. The chapter concludes by offering discussion strategies that span across subject areas.

Chapter 3 challenges the ways that research traditionally is conceptualized in school and society—including the focus on objectivity, adult expertise, and distance. In the chapter I discuss my experience coordinating a youth participatory action research (YPAR) collaborative with high school students and teachers in Los Angeles, as well as integrating YPAR into my own English classroom. I explore how situating young people as experts of their own experiences and encouraging their curiosity about the challenges they see around them can revolutionize the research experience in ways that cultivate critical civic empathy. I analyze how participatory research lifts up previously marginalized voices and encourages students to involve themselves in both naming and solving social inequities through critical literacy skills. The chapter concludes by stressing the need to support young people as civic agents and the subjects (rather than objects) of educational and social reforms.

In Chapter 4, I analyze the ways that students use digital media both in- and outside of school spaces to express themselves and forge their civic identities in an increasingly multimodal public sphere. I offer connected learning as a framework for approaching digital literacy education in ways that encourage student interest, collaboration, and critical civic empathy, and highlight the work of teachers in the National Writing Project network who are exemplifying what it takes to be a connected teacher. The chapter concludes by highlighting the possibilities of critical digital literacy to reinvigorate civic life, countering critics' claims that digital technology has eroded empathy.

Chapter 5 acknowledges the need for us to think in new ways about our identities as teachers if we are to embrace critical civic empathy as a guiding principle for literacy education. I explore the need for teachers to consider their own civic identities and interrogate their beliefs about the purpose of literacy education before they begin building their curricula, in order to lend focus and social consciousness to their literacy instruction. I discuss two surveys that I was involved in creating, which found that English teachers are juggling multiple goals for their instruction and are more likely to integrate current events into their practice if they themselves are more civically engaged outside of work. I share stories from teachers I have worked with about how they think about themselves as civic agents and how their commitments as citizens influence their classroom practice. The chapter concludes with recommendations for teachers about how to stay focused on civic purpose amid accountability demands.

Finally, the Conclusion reviews the concept of critical civic empathy and the possibilities for instilling this disposition in students through a variety of critical literacy practices in both formal and informal learning spaces. I repeat the crucial need for empathy if we are to face the challenges of the 21st century together as a democratic society and offer recommendations for policy and practice that can make it easier for educators and students to integrate civic consciousness into schooling. I conclude with the hope that literacy education can be used as a force for joy and justice in public life.

Through this text, I aim to contribute to the field of literacy education by provoking dialogue about the relationship between schooling and society and the kinds of citizens we want our students to become—and then offering ways forward in research, policy, and practice.

CHAPTER 1

Warrior-Scholars and Bridge-Builders

Honing the Social Imagination
Through Literary Analysis

"Without literature, life is hell."

—Charles Bukowski

I think many English teachers would agree that Bukowski was on to something here. While he *might* indulge in a bit of hyperbole with his fire-and-brimstone imagery, he makes a vivid argument about the crucial role that literature plays in enriching the lives of those who read it. English teachers have been making this argument in some form or another since what seems like the beginning of time (or at least since English became a core high school subject at the turn of the 20th century) to justify the place of literary texts in the English language arts (ELA) curriculum.

To get a sense of exactly how important the teaching of literature is to English teachers, consider the firestorm that emerged during the rollout of the ELA Common Core State Standards, when the shifting focus toward analysis of informational texts led many to believe that the standards intended to eliminate the teaching of fiction from English classrooms altogether. Dozens of think pieces sounded the alarm across the blogosphere, including one on the Huffington Post ominously titled "Common Core and the Death of Reading." *U.S. News & World Report* published a special report breathlessly detailing the "content and controversy." The architects of the standards quickly sought to dispel the "myth" that fiction was about to be knocked off its prized pedestal in English classrooms, but a transition clearly had begun.

The issue has shaken many teachers and teacher educators to their core by destabilizing their long-held beliefs about the centrality of literature to the English curriculum, but it also raises some crucial questions for the field that need to be considered. As I see it, the most important one is: What are we fighting for? What *exactly* is it that our students gain from reading and responding to literature that makes the practice so essential to our discipline? We must be able to offer a clear and compelling answer to this question in order to both preserve literary analysis as a key competency in our subject amid shifting priorities *and* guide our planning about which texts to teach (and how to teach them) in purposeful ways.

In this chapter, I will highlight the development of critical civic empathy as a particularly compelling rationale for teaching literature—one that focuses on preparing students to participate thoughtfully and compassionately in 21st-century society. I will share the practices of two high school English teachers in Los Angeles in order to demonstrate how literature can not only reflect our own experiences back to us and offer windows into the experiences of others, but also ultimately construct bridges with the power to connect us in public life. This exploration will help us consider more deeply exactly what Paulo Freire meant when he talked about the connection between reading *the word* and reading *the world*.

WHY TEACH LITERATURE IN THE ENGLISH CLASSROOM? (AND WHAT EXACTLY COUNTS AS LITERATURE, ANYWAY?)

So, how exactly can literature save our students from the hellish life of Bukowski's imagination? The idea that reading literature somehow makes us better people stands out among many English teachers as the most nebulous but also most deeply felt rationale for teaching literary texts in schools (Zunshine, 2006). The problem is that it is difficult to pinpoint exactly what aspects of character are enriched by literature and how literature achieves this enrichment. Not surprisingly, the group that can be reliably counted upon for making grand but vague pronouncements about what literature adds to our lives are authors themselves. Consider this quote from novelist Anne Lamott (1995):

> What a miracle it is that out of these small, flat, rigid squares of paper unfolds world after world after world, worlds that sing to you, comfort and quiet or excite you. Books help us understand who we are and how we are to behave. They show us what community and friendship mean; they show us how to live and die. (p. 15)

I can imagine that the voracious readers out there are nodding their heads, like me, in visceral agreement with this sentiment; nevertheless, to an administrator or policymaker, this argument might not sound very convincing without a little more specificity. Fortunately, a number of psychologists and neuroscientists recently have stepped forward with attempts to specify exactly *how* literature opens the gateway to self-discovery, community, and friendship—and they have zeroed in on the concept of empathy.

Although difficult to gauge precisely, recent scientific experiments have sought to measure empathy through surveys (a popular questionnaire, the Interpersonal Reactivity Index, includes items such as "I sometimes try to understand my friends better by imagining how things look from their perspective") and tests (one involves looking at pictures of people's eyes and trying to determine their emotions). Many of these experiments have concluded that folks who frequently read literature score higher on measures of empathy than those who do not (Bal & Veltkamp, 2013; Mar & Oatley, 2008).

The prevalent explanation for this relationship between literature and empathy is that engaging with stories fosters the ability to understand the beliefs, experiences, and perspectives of others—what cognitive psychologists call theory of mind. As Keith Oatley (2016), one of those exploring the relationship between fiction and empathy, puts it, "Fiction can be thought of as a form of consciousness of selves and others that can be passed from an author to a reader or spectator, and can be internalized to augment everyday cognition" (p. 618). Or, as we educators might put it, reading stories that plunge us into the hearts and minds of fictional characters and allow us see the world through their eyes enlarges our own perspectives and helps us approach *real* people with newfound humility and compassion.

Disagreements have emerged, however, over what kind of literature might best foster empathy. While some argue that form is not a crucial factor—that immersive television shows or video games could have the same benefits as novels—others contend that "literary" fiction is more likely to elicit theory of mind than "popular" fiction or other text genres (Kidd & Castano, 2013). Thus, I suggest that we pause for a moment to consider the age-old question of what counts as literature. I argue that if our purpose in teaching literature is to offer students expansive visions of possible democratic futures, we must embrace an expansive vision of literature itself. But let's outline exactly why.

In order to do so, we must consider anew the Western literary canon—the reason behind why you'll find copies of particular novels (e.g., *To Kill a Mockingbird, The Great Gatsby*) in nearly every school book room in the country. Decades after these books were published, a confluence of authors, intellectuals, and educators decided that they belonged in the canon of American literature and, in turn, that the youth of America should read and experience them as common cultural touchstones.

The idea undergirding the canon is that a work of literature reflects the country/culture in which it is produced—its successes, its failures, its best ideas and enduring tensions—while also speaking to universal human themes (Bloom, 1994). And some works are thought to capture such powerful reflections that they embody a particular essence of a time and place; these are the texts that some propose should be read widely in order to foster a shared cultural experience or common cultural vocabulary.

Of course, as long as the idea of a literary canon has existed, so has the debate over what should be included in it and what value it has in a society characterized by diversity of every social category and experience. Here in the United States, critics argue that the canon inappropriately privileges particular stories as representative of American culture when, in fact, no single American culture exists; as such, its very existence serves to marginalize stories that deviate from those told by people in positions of power (Guillory, 1993).

Further, the canon also is seen as seeking to categorize and foster divisions between forms of creative expression—between literary and popular fiction, "high" and "low" art. If you have texts like *Maus* or *Persepolis* in your school curriculum—graphic novels that combine storytelling with imagery and comic-book formatting—those were likely recent and hard-won purchases due to the controversy over whether alternative format texts "count" as literature. In fact, if you have personally experienced or heard about controversies erupting at schools about the propriety of particular texts to be taught in English classes, these flare-ups are likely to be related at least partially to tensions over what qualifies as literature.

I feel the need to push on the ways that strict adherence to the idea of a canon is contrary to the spirit of empathy and suggest that a critical civic perspective can help us clarify a greater purpose for our field—one focused on creating not just good people, but also good citizens in a complex, 21st-century democracy. I argue that literary texts—conceptualized in the most expansive way possible—have a powerful role to play in this process, one that I want to explore by introducing some important literary thinkers and then showcasing some transformative classroom practices.

FROM EMPATHY TO CRITICAL CIVIC EMPATHY: THE ROLE OF LITERATURE

In contrast to psychological studies, which adhere to an individual model of empathy, I am interested in using the concept of critical civic empathy to push the dialogue toward recognizing ourselves (and other individuals) within a political context as members of socially constructed groups with different levels of power and privilege, while reimagining caring in terms of engagement with public life. Within this model, reading literature can become a mutually humanizing experience that can spur social action. Here's how it works: Students, as members of multiple and overlapping social groups, sit down with a novel (a political artifact in its own right), identify with characters who represent groups to which they may or may not belong, and take these identifications out into the world with them as they interact with fellow citizens and make decisions about social issues that impact us all.

Literary texts are particularly powerful tools for the development of critical civic empathy for many of the same reasons we just noted—they explore particular social and cultural tensions through the eyes of characters that readers can relate to—but also because their creative form offers openings through which readers can break away from cold, hard facts and the seeming intractability of the way things are, to imagine new and different possibilities for society. I want to explore the work of various thinkers who push us to consider these ideas in tandem—first, the idea of literature as civic text; and second, the acts of reading and writing as civic engagement.

Toni Morrison, one of America's greatest literary treasures, helps us understand how literary texts stand as primary source documents that are just as powerful as factual accounts in illuminating current events and social tensions. In her essay in *Playing in the Dark: Whiteness and the Literary Imagination*, Morrison (1992) starts from the premise that literature "ends up describing and inscribing what is really on the national mind" (p. 15). She then focuses her attention specifically on American literature in order to contend that one of the most pressing issues on our national mind is race and the African American experience. She takes the reader through the work of numerous American writers, from Willa Cather to Edgar Allan Poe to Ernest Hemingway, to offer her critical take on how race is treated and how African American characters are delineated in plotlines and themes—at the same time revealing the personal impetus behind the composition of her own masterpieces.

Most important, Morrison (1992) makes the connection between the creative process and civic action; as she explains:

> Living in a nation of people who *decided* that their world view would combine agendas for individual freedom *and* mechanisms for devastating racial oppression presents a singular landscape for a writer. When this world view is taken seriously as agency, the literature produced within and without it offers an unprecedented opportunity to comprehend the resilience and gravity, the inadequacy and the force of the imaginative act. (p. xiii, emphasis original)

In this passage, Morrison (1992) portrays writers as complex civic actors and identifies writing as an act of imaginative agency that necessarily grapples with civic issues. Morrison views authors as respondents to culture, constantly criticizing, valorizing, and transforming the world through their imaginative work, and she believes that through reading, readers become authors as well, engaging in the same political activities. When we read literature, we are participating in the civic struggle of the author and contributing to the narrative. In fact, Morrison argues that reading literature in a way that exposes cultural and political assumptions transforms knowledge from a force of "invasion and conquest" to one of "revelation and choice" (p. 8). This type of reading, as she puts it, does not involve "merely looking or looking at," but "becoming" (p. 4)—representing the movement from sympathy to empathy.

Philosophers have continued to explore the civic potential of the act of reading literature; for example, political theorist Martha Nussbaum (1997) argues that literary analysis should be required of lawyers and judges so that their decisions can be based on a more complex, humanistic view of the individuals whose lives they often hold in their hands rather than the narrow, economically deterministic model that often prevails in public policy.

And, most important to us teachers, educational philosopher Maxine Greene (2000) makes the case for a civic approach to classroom study of literature. She argues that reading allows young people to "discover ordinarily unseen and unknown dimensions of their own experiences" and that, as a result, "not only may there be a pull toward new relationships, toward community, but such readers may be moved also to new modes of self-definition, new beginnings arising from an emerging awareness of both difference and possibility" (p. 42). Greene sees these new beginnings as social as well as personal, suggesting possibilities for changing the world and ourselves. She explains that classroom dialogue about texts releases the "social imagination," which she defines as "the capacity to invent visions of what should be and what might be in our deficient society, on the streets where we live, in our schools" (p. 5).

Greene's conception of imagination as a creative social construct as well as a personal artistic one directly contributes to my model of critical civic empathy because it acknowledges that reading and responding to literature can be a step toward concrete social action. It is through interaction with stories that provoke personal identification that students can analyze the social, historical, and political discourses that structure both their societies and their lives. I argue that literature gives young people the creative license to imagine a world different from the one they live in, and that imagining the experiences of other citizens and of a more just world is a crucial first step to making such a world a reality.

Deborah Appleman, an influential English educator, put these theories into practice and demonstrated that middle and high school students are capable of reading texts as social artifacts as well as purely literary ones. In her groundbreaking book (now in its second edition), *Critical Encounters in High School English: Teaching Literary Theory to Adolescents*, Appleman (2009) provided classroom stories to illuminate how encouraging students to evaluate literary texts through the lenses of critical social theories, from feminism to postcolonialism to Marxism, allowed them to simultaneously analyze literature *and* society. Importantly, she did not discount students' personal connections to texts; rather, she situated these connections within the broader context of reader-response theory and teased out the interactions between the personal and public that play out each time we pick up a novel or delve into a poem.

Let's synthesize how critical civic empathy can manifest itself through the critical literacy practice of literary response and analysis. The critical aspect emerges from the use of social theories to interrogate literary texts and from reflection about our positionality as members of social groups that we bring to our experience of reading. The civic aspect highlights the ways that literary texts contribute to discussions about current social issues and can jumpstart discussions about opportunities for public engagement to address these issues. These modifiers help define empathy as a process of activating the social imagination and creatively embodying new civic possibilities.

And importantly, no particular texts—canonical or otherwise—have a monopoly on eliciting these connections. I turn to Maxine Greene (2000) for wisdom once again because she provides an expansive definition of literature appropriate for fostering the social imagination and critical civic empathy in the 21st-century classroom (and society). Greene defines imaginative literature as any text that "resonates" because "the words mean more than they denote, evoking in those willing to pay heed other images, memories, things desired, things lost, things never entirely grasped or understood" (p. 44). This definition, with its focus on the kind of thinking that texts inspire rather than their forms, helps us transcend the culture wars over the canon and instead maintain a focus on the habits of mind that creative work can inspire.

Let's now turn toward exploring how English teachers can integrate literary texts into their curriculum in different ways that both meet academic standards and inspire critical civic empathy.

LITERARY ANALYSIS IN THE CLASSROOM:
TEACHER CASE STUDIES

While I was working on my doctorate, I coordinated an after-school youth civic engagement program at the University of California, Los Angeles (more on that to come in Chapter 3). The experiences that the participating high school students had in the program, as they put their literacy skills to work in researching and addressing social issues in their communities, caused many of them to wonder why they didn't get to learn in this transformative way in school. As Timothy, one of our students, put it, "If my English class was like this, I'd actually like it."

As an English teacher, I was stung by Timothy's comment. Though I had to acknowledge that perhaps not enough English classes were making connections to civic life, I knew that many were. I decided that I wanted to study the practices of English teachers who consciously sought to connect their subject matter to democratic engagement in order to highlight classroom possibilities, even in a context of accountability pressures and student academic struggle. Through a series of focus groups with students in my after-school program, I learned about two 10th-grade English teachers who fit the bill of what I was looking for: Jerica Coffey, a 10-year veteran who taught at a public charter high school in South Los Angeles, and Ashley Englander, a 6th-year teacher who taught at a traditional public high school in East Los Angeles. Both schools served large populations of students of color living in poverty and both struggled to meet their annual accountability goals.

I collaborated with Jerica and Ashley to develop a study about how they brought commitments to democratic engagement to their practice as English teachers. I share some of their practices related to literary analysis here in order to illustrate the multiplicity of ways that English teachers can infuse public life into their curriculum and instruction in ways that foster critical civic empathy in their students. These portraits are meant to spark reflection and discussion about how more teachers can develop their own identities as critical literacy educators.

The Warrior-Scholar

During the first few minutes of the first day I observed Jerica's 1st-period, 10th-grade ELA class, as I situated myself in the back of the room and glanced at the writing prompt displayed on the whiteboard, I heard her say to her students, "If your pen is not to your page, you are not handling your business as a warrior-scholar."

I was immediately intrigued by this term and wrote a note reminding myself to ask her what it meant—particularly because it seemed that students had become accustomed to it and understood its significance. Indeed, over the course of my time in Jerica's class, the term *warrior-scholar* came up dozens of times. It was used alternately as a form of encouragement ("You've gotta stand up and read it. That's real warrior-scholar status.") and a form of praise ("I appreciate you stepping up like a warrior-scholar.").

When I asked Jerica about the origin and meaning of warrior-scholarship, she explained that she developed this concept as a way to communicate to students her commitment to a vision of literacy linked to self- and social empowerment. She described working with a self-organized group of like-minded educators the summer before the start of the school year to figure out ways to increase student engagement. Through those conversations, she decided to identify students as warrior-scholars as "a culture piece that's establishing a sense of purpose." She elaborated forcefully about how she sees that purpose:

> What it did was it allowed me to communicate my philosophy of education. On the first day of school, I was like, you know what, I'm not here to just teach. Screw that. What matters is that you're going to use this, you're going to fight for your people, and you're going to use this to change what's going on in your communities. And that's why I'm here. So I think it has helped a lot for them to understand . . . why we're doing what we do, and the sense of urgency that they need to have.

Jerica articulated a very clear vision for student learning grounded in collective identity and community action. Students seemed to internalize the concept of warrior-scholarship over the course of the school year and played with the idea of truly seeing themselves as warrior-scholars. When I asked one student, Carlos, what the term meant to him, he responded, "I think it's about getting our education and helping our community instead of just trying to get out. To do better and give back." He grinned shyly when I asked him if he considered himself a warrior-scholar, responding, "I'm getting there." Another student, Stephanie, told me that to be at that level, "you don't punk out on your community. You try your best with your work. You're the leader, and you try to do the right things."

All of the students I talked to considered "warrior-scholar status" something to aspire to and saw themselves getting closer to fulfilling its promise when they committed themselves to their academic work. The fact that mundane classroom behaviors such as bringing books to class and completing homework could be indicative of warrior-scholarship, just as much as challenging inequality, points to the way that Jerica connected every aspect of academic success to a responsibility to the community—things we do for "our hood."

Jerica translated her commitment to empowering education and social justice into concrete literacy practices in her classroom. Often, just a simple shift in the set-up or naming of an activity could turn a traditional academic literacy into one imbued with more critical meanings. For instance, Ms. Coffey told me that when she was in school, she loved to read; however, her teachers did not make her feel like her opinions about texts mattered. As she explained, "It wasn't in that way where I have something to bring to the table, to this conversation." As a result, when she got to college and was asked what she thought of a text, she described her reaction as, "What do I have to say that's important?" These experiences contributed to the way she introduced texts in her class; as she stated:

> My conviction is to make sure that young folks don't feel that way. Young people have to access these dominant texts, but the vehicle has to be something that speaks to them and humanizes them and makes them feel valuable, because otherwise, you'll never get them to read the difficult stuff.

Jerica carefully chose literature that reflected many of the social issues that her students were facing in their community. She explained that after establishing the theoretical focus for a unit, she immediately turned to choosing the texts that will ground it; as she put it, "I start there, what are the theories that I want to expose them to, and then kind of work backwards from there. What are the texts that I feel strongly about? I feel strongly about all the texts that I've used."

One such important text for her was *Our America*, which Ms. Coffey used as the central text for a unit about juvenile justice. The nonfiction book was written by two teenagers, LeAlan Jones and Lloyd Newman (Jones, Newman, Isay, 1998), as they sought to understand the death of a 5-year-old boy from their Chicago neighborhood at the hands of two boys only a few years older than him. LeAlan's epigraph reads, "You must learn our America as we must learn your America, so that, maybe, someday, we can become one." In the preface, Cornel West praised the book for providing counter-narratives to prevailing stereotypes about young Black men, noting how infrequently society hears "the poignant and powerful voices of these fellow citizens."

Throughout my observations, the students in Ms. Coffey's class were thoroughly absorbed in LeAlan and Lloyd's narratives. Students had multiple opportunities to connect with the book in ways that helped them articulate opinions on social issues. Ms. Coffey phrased the essential question for the unit using a collective pronoun that invited identification with the text; she asked students, "Are we products of our environment, or do we have the power to shape our lives?"

Over time, I noticed that while students were using evidence from the text to explore the context of poverty and violence within which two young boys killed Eric Morse, they also were analyzing the societal factors that influenced their own lives. Carlos made a personal connection to the text and to the oppressive circumstances facing children living in Chicago's South Side when he said, "I think that we have a choice. I grew up in a rough neighborhood as well as they did and I'm not out killing people or gang-banging." Another student, Derek, made a similar connection to the text as he vehemently rejected the idea that social forces could have an impact on his choices in life: "You won't hear me on the street saying it's because of my environment that I'm doing the stuff I'm doing. It really does not matter." In both cases, the students not only demonstrated personal connections to the text by distinguishing the choices they made from those the characters made, but also wrestled with the impact that discourses about poverty and its possible consequences could have on their own lives through their references to their "rough neighborhood."

I found that students often went beyond creating simple text-to-self connections to engaging with the bigger social problems raised by these texts. This was due to conscious decisions made by Jerica to choose texts that she found relevant to what students experienced around them; as she explained, "I thought it would engage students to talk about things going on in the community, and to read some things about what's going on in the community."

She teamed up with another English teacher in her department for the juvenile justice unit, and after both classes had read *Our America*, they each created a case for why the two young men who committed murder should be tried for their crime either as adults or as juveniles. Jerica and her colleague recruited other teachers in the school to serve as judges, and the classes engaged in a full mock trial, complete with student lawyers, witnesses, and jury members. Students learned how to support their claims with evidence in order to present compelling cases to others and how to pick apart counter evidence for weaknesses. Students then translated these skills back to academic writing when they used their cases as the basis for persuasive essays, effectively bridging the realms of school and civic life.

Jerica also used the ELA standard related to business letters to develop an assignment bridging academic literacy, civic engagement, and social critique by having students write letters about their concerns with California's juvenile justice system to the state's governor, Jerry Brown. Jerica intended this assignment to give students a chance to integrate what they had learned about the prison industrial complex with their literacy skills in order to take concrete action in the real world. These letters represented, in a sense, the fulfillment of Jerica's teaching philosophy—they combined a commitment to community empowerment with social awareness while showcasing students' literacy skills. It seems fitting to summarize the constructions of literacy and citizenship that Jerica and her students developed by sharing the content of one of these letters:

> Dear Honorable Jerry Brown:
> I have many concerns about the society we live in. I am truly disappointed with our juvenile justice system. You should take into consideration that with all the money being wasted in prisons, we could use it for something more important—for instance, our schools. With all that money we can motivate our children to stay in school instead of being guided into the wrong path.
> If it were up to me to make that difficult decision, I would recommend that we lower prison funds and raise the school fund. For example, to incarcerate a young person it costs $234,000 per year. Instead, we can be using all that money to help the youth become better people. You as the governor can provide us with rehabilitation programs so that teens can get the help needed.
> We as the community are trying to encourage you to spend that money on better school supplies, counselors to help guide the children, and after-school programs to give youth the tools to be successful in life instead of getting into a life full of crime and bad influences.
> Sincerely,
> Irene

The Bridge-Builder

It was only my third day of observation with Ashley and the 10th-grade students in her 5th-period ELA class; I was still learning students' names and trying to remember my way through the vast campus to get to the correct room. Ashley's room was located outside of the main building within a maze of portable classrooms, and although it usually took students a few extra minutes to walk over to it, there was something refreshing about a class-room that opened up to fresh air and sunshine. Ashley stood in the doorway and made a point of shaking hands with each of the students as they entered the room, looking them in the eye with a smile and saying hello. Students grinned shyly back at her and then made their way to their seats.

A nervous energy permeated the room on this particular day, for stu-dents were preparing to recite original poems in front of their classmates as the culmination of a poetry analysis unit. They mouthed words to them-selves as they signed up on the performance list and fidgeted at their desks. Ashley began the class by reminding students that they would be providing feedback to one another after the poems were read, and then asked Luis to serve as the emcee for the day. He bounded to the front of the room with a smile and began calling students up to the "stage," exhorting his peers to applaud for each poet. It became apparent very quickly that students felt safe enough to share deeply personal feelings with the class; while some read upbeat poems about friendship or pride in themselves, many more tackled troubling issues ranging from loneliness to racism. After each reading, stu-dents praised one another's work, thoughtfully pointing out lines they liked and images they found especially powerful. The caring atmosphere in the room immediately struck me; I was impressed by the way that students sub-tly supported one another emotionally.

The idea of connection seemed key to Ashley's teaching philosophy; as in the poetry assignment, in which students analyzed famous poems and then used the writing styles they had learned in order to construct their own original work, Ashley consistently encouraged students to make connec-tions among one another and between themselves and the outside world. In our conversations, she explicitly related this idea of connection to her view of citizenship; as she explained, "I think that probably the main thing I do as a good citizen is that I'm a bit of a bridge-builder. I definitely have the privilege of being in a few different communities at once, as far as being not a resident of, but a member of the East Los Angeles community." In her teaching practice, Ashley manifested a commitment to caring deeply for her students and the neighborhood in which they lived. She carved out a role for herself as a "bridge-builder" to connect them with a larger community through literacy.

Ashley described the questions that she would ask herself while plan-ning units and the texts that she selected: "What will engage their diverse reading levels and interests? And then also what will make them more so-cially aware? Texts that will make them more critical of the world and crit-ical of society, but also texts that reflect their own life enough that they are engaged by it."

Most of the literacy practices that I observed in Ashley's classroom during the last few months of the school year revolved around the study of *Night*, Elie Wiesel's Holocaust memoir, and its themes of oppression and resistance. Ashley chose this text in collaboration with the 10th-grade world history teacher as they planned an interdisciplinary humanities unit about World War II. Ashley saw the integration of literacy and history curriculum as a way to further help students use their language skills to make connections between different subject areas and critically analyze their society. The essential questions that she developed for this unit included:

- What is oppression, and how can we identify and recognize oppression?
- How do people resist oppression?
- What are the steps to genocide?
- Why do people bystand and why do they intervene?

Ashley's goal in this unit was not simply to help students understand oppression and resistance in an historical context through the study of the Holocaust, but also to help them identify current examples of oppression and resistance in their lives in order to facilitate social change. As a result, while the unit opened with the study of *Night*, it concluded with an analysis of an educational research article that Ashley used to provoke discussion about the role of schools as institutions of either marginalization or empowerment for students.

Ashley chose to introduce this unit with a simulation activity designed to provide students with a visceral experience to illustrate the complexities of bystanding and intervening in the face of oppression. My fieldnotes for that day recount the dramatic event:

Ashley walks to the back of the room and picks up a small fish tank with two live goldfish in it. As she carries it to the front of the room, students start to comment on the goldfish. Ashley says nothing—simply puts the tank down on a stool, opens the top, catches one of the fish with a net, and takes it out of the bowl, placing it on the ground. Students yell, "What are you doing?" Some gasp. Others ask what is going on. Jesus says, "I'm going to save it." Others simply look on, dumbfounded and confused. He gets out of his seat and picks the struggling fish up off the floor, gently placing it back in the tank safely. Once Jesus puts the fish back in the bowl, Ashley tells everyone to give him a round of applause. Eddie asks, "Was this a joke?" Ashley tells everyone not to say anything yet, instead motioning to the chart paper stand next to the whiteboard, where the following questions are written down, "What were you thinking? What were you feeling?"

After students spent several minutes writing, Ashley elicited their responses. Celeste said, "I hated you. I was wondering, what if no one saved it?" Jesus said, "I was shocked." Sergio added, "I didn't think you would do something like that." As students recounted their feelings and discussed the reasons why they did not stand up to save the fish, instead waiting for someone else to do something, Kevin noticed that the words *World War II* were written on the board and began to understand the rationale for the activity. He told the class, "This is about how people stood by as Jewish people were killed during the Holocaust."

At this point, Ashley introduced the essential questions for the unit, as well as the final essay prompt that students would be tackling at the end of it about how Nazi oppression functioned and how Jewish people resisted. She told students that the purpose of the simulation was to connect the events of the Holocaust to ongoing questions about "human psychology"; as she explained, "It's not necessarily that bystanding is bad and intervening is good. It's not that simple. You can think in life about when you should step in and when you should not. The goal is that next time you get into a situation you'll think about it." With this statement, Ashley made an explicit connection for her students between the literacy practices they would engage in throughout this unit and the future choices that they would make in their everyday lives about universal themes of oppression and resistance. Indeed, students immediately began relating these themes to their lives, thinking about when they would get involved to stop wrongdoing and when they would hold back.

This unit provided multiple examples of Ashley's teaching philosophy in action—moments when literacy skills were used in the service of helping students articulate their opinions and beliefs about ongoing social issues and how people should interact in a just society. Students analyzed primary documents, including pieces of Nazi propaganda, an American propaganda film, and articles drawn from the popular Facing History and Ourselves curriculum, not only as an academic exercise designed to help them develop evidence for their essay writing, but also as a means of asking philosophical questions about human nature and our capacity for cruelty toward others perceived as different. Several weeks into the unit, pieces of chart paper covered the walls of the room containing questions that students had that could not be easily answered: How could humans do this? What if there was no Hitler? What happened to the survivors? How did the Nazis live with what they'd done?

Their close textual analysis helped students eventually produce strong analytic essays about oppression and resistance during World War II; in addition, it provided students with the skills needed to turn their lens on the current educational system and look for ways that similar themes of oppression and resistance emerged in their school.

Before introducing students to the academic article about forms of student resistance to oppressive schooling conditions, Ashley asked students for their own opinions about how students could be marginalized in schools and what their responses could be. She set up pieces of chart paper around the room and asked students to walk around and write down their answers to these questions, putting a check mark next to another student's idea if they agreed. Students' responses revealed a great deal of critical thinking about the struggles students face in and out of the classroom.

They were able to identify social and institutional forces that negatively impact student success, from racism to school resources to bad teachers, and then recognize the self-destructive (e.g., drugs and alcohol) and empowering (e.g., self-confidence) ways that students could exert agency over these forces. Ashley brought the unit full circle by having students consider how Elie Wiesel might have responded to these conditions and write about transformative possibilities for combating current-day oppression in and out of school.

DISCUSSION: CRITICAL CIVIC EMPATHY IN ACTION

Imaginative texts sparked discussions and writing in Jerica's and Ashley's classrooms that went beyond simple text-to-self or text-to-world connections. For these teachers, critical literacy involved interrogation of texts and the social context in which they are written—the kind of interrogation that I argue is crucial to the development of critical civic empathy that both teachers pursued.

This is not to say, of course, that critical literacy and critical civic education should be considered monolithic entities that dictate particular viewpoints and classroom activities for English teachers. These portraits indicate that teachers who share conscious commitments to literacy as a tool for civic empowerment nevertheless manifest these commitments in myriad ways. The warrior-scholar, Jerica, focused on the ways that literacy could help students understand forms of oppression in their lives and speak out in protest and resistance, whereas the bridge-builder, Ashley, committed herself to the practice of helping students gain access to codes of power through language and connect with dominant communities. Of course, there was a great deal of overlap between their practices, as well; my point is that each maintained strong and identifiable points of view in the classroom that could be traced to her unique personal and social contexts but that shared common commitments to mutual humanization among students and the larger society.

Yet, central to my analysis of critical civic empathy is the idea that the way students are positioned in society is key to understanding how they develop civic political and civic identities. The social context in which they live—one that, for urban students of color, often is characterized by marginalization and alienation—inevitably influences their attitudes toward social institutions and democratic governance. Both of my focus teachers integrated this social context into the curriculum and pedagogy of their classes—it influenced the texts they introduced to students, the topics they offered for discussion, and the ways they moderated classroom talk. Most important, however, this social context influenced the ways that the teachers viewed the purposes of literacy instruction. They based their pedagogy in the idea that language represented a tool that could help students not simply to understand themselves and their society, but to transform their lives and society as well. As students toyed with opinions about social issues and struggled with the inequalities of our current world, we clearly could see them imagining the ideal selves they wanted to become and the ideal society they wanted to inhabit. Discussions about literature allowed students to construct visions of a better democracy that teachers hoped literacy would help them to achieve through social action.

Richard Beach (2005) explains the ways in which students' interactions with literary texts reflect their interactions with society: "In experiencing characters interrogating ideological forces limiting their development, students began to examine forces in their own lives limiting their own development" (p. 1). He argues that critical response to literature should involve an emphasis on "the ways in which the reading transaction is mediated by discourses, genres, narrative, language, and intertextuality operating in particular historical and cultural contexts" (p. 2).

In both teachers' classrooms, the students were not simply reading and discussing imaginative texts; instead, they were analyzing them as social and cultural artifacts transmitting ideas about race and class that they then reinterpreted themselves based on their lived experiences in society.

Literary texts, through their creative forms, draw students into compelling narrative worlds. These imaginative worlds hold up a mirror so that students can analyze the real world in which they live. This analysis helps them think about social problems and gives them creative license to think about changing the world for the better. It is this sense of possibility and linguistic play that leads classroom literacy researchers like Jeffrey Wilhelm (2008) to see imaginative texts as profoundly democratic works of art. As he explains, "[Literature] questions the way the world is and offers possibilities for the way it could be. It offers a variety of views, visions, and voices that are so vital to a democracy. Literature helps us to define ourselves as we are, and to envision what we want ourselves and the world to be" (p. 53). These texts helped the students in Jerica's and Ashley's classrooms develop their social imaginations and picture different possibilities for society and themselves through civically engaged literacy experiences—the key to critical civic empathy.

CONCLUSION

In this chapter, I have argued that literary analysis is a unique disciplinary practice that makes English classrooms potentially powerful sites of civic learning, largely because of the ways that literature can spur imaginative thinking about social issues and provide students with agency to think about new possibilities for our society. I have demonstrated how teachers can use literary analysis to foster critical civic empathy in their students through several steps:

1. Considering their own teaching philosophies and their students' civic positioning and experiences
2. Using these considerations to structure civically engaged essential questions to guide classroom literacy activities
3. Carefully choosing literary texts that tackle civic issues and engage with students by reflecting, extending, or challenging their identities and experiences
4. Offering opportunities for students to respond to literature in authentic and civically engaged ways

In order to remind myself to incorporate a focus on civic engagement into every element of my unit planning process, from the essential questions to the assessments, I created a template for civically engaged unit planning (see Appendix A). The simple design prompts me to think about the ways I can make sure that each of my formative and summative assessments incorporates at least one nod to civic learning and that my text sets exemplify a range of perspectives and identities. I start my planning by naming the knowledge and skills that I want students to demonstrate by the end of the unit, so that I can then plan backward to ensure that I design lessons that help students build toward these goals. This template provides a structured way for me to continuously think about ways to foster critical civic empathy that I hope can be useful to you in your planning.

In the poem "Asphodel, That Greeny Flower," American poet William Carlos Williams (1955) wrote, "It is difficult to get the news from poems, but men die miserably every day from lack of what is found there" (p. 55). It can be difficult indeed to connect the study of literature to the enactment of citizenship and "get the news" from poems, but Williams's quote demonstrates the urgency of doing so in order to make our personal and public lives more meaningful. Williams poignantly illustrates the devastating and dehumanizing effects that come from ignoring the immediacy of literature to our daily lives as citizens. The stories that we tell of ourselves and of our nation are inextricably wound up in the stories composed by our fellow citizens. Without a critical civic pedagogy in English classrooms, literacy will remain isolated from our civic life, and civic life, in turn, will remain unimaginative and restricted to dominant forms of engagement. We have a role to play in disrupting that narrative and forging a new one.

DISCUSSION/REFLECTION QUESTIONS

1. How do you think that literary texts are positioned in your classroom/ department/school? Canonical texts for students to appreciate? Models of good writing? Catalysts for empathy? Something more?

2. Consider the literature that you love to teach. How could these texts connect to current events and civic issues?

3. How could you develop critical literacy opportunities for your students grounded in literary analysis that help students analyze the world and their places within it?

4. What goals do you have for developing critical civic empathy in your students through literary analysis?

CHAPTER 2

Three Sides to Every Story
Civic Communication Through Debate

In some ways, debate seems like a constant in today's political discourse; nearly every newsworthy occurrence or policy proposal that pops up immediately sparks ferocious verbal sparring between individuals on opposite sides of increasingly vast partisan divides. Whether in more formal settings like congressional chambers and press conferences or informal environments like Twitter or cable news, Americans appear to be debating all the time.

And yet, this description does not feel quite accurate. Debates possess certain standards of mutual respect, discourse, and structure that separate them from arguments or fights, and those standards often are deteriorating or absent today. First, as discussed in the Introduction, our country's polarization reaches beyond differences of ideas to battles over identity; instead of disagreements about issues, we are experiencing fundamental differences over whose country this is. The renewed boldness of White supremacist groups and the populist "us versus them" rhetoric of "taking the country back" from minoritized groups of Americans create an untenable situation for debate; true debate cannot take place when one participant refuses to recognize the very humanity of the other. This dehumanizing atmosphere is seeping into schools; in a nationally representative survey of educators, researcher John Rogers and colleagues (2017) found that incivility and reliance on unsubstantiated sources are rising in classrooms in the wake of the 2016 U.S. presidential election, particularly in predominantly White schools as White students denigrate peers from racially and religiously minoritized groups.

Second, just as debate requires baseline levels of respect, so does it require a shared foundation of fact; while opponents do not necessarily need to agree on the nature of the problem under discussion or the best ways to address it, they at least need to agree on the validity of the information being brought to bear as evidence. When we switch between different cable news channels, it sometimes seems as if anchors and pundits are operating on different planes of reality in discussing the same event, their basic understanding of major points of fact so far apart as to render any attempt at dialogue impossible. As discussed earlier, the splintering of the media ecology has encouraged us to seek out information that confirms our framing of the world and remain ensconced in our ideological echo chambers. Add to that the proliferation of fake news and the blatant attempts to undermine democratic norms by agents both foreign and domestic, and a common ground for discussion feels shaky indeed.

Finally, the rules and format of debate can feel outdated at a time when public discourse flows in all directions and in multiple formats through tweets, videos, and other curated social media posts. Debate can conjure images of stodgy politicians at lecterns stuck in the past as discourse bounces around the world with the touch of a button. In addition, the competitive nature of debate can seem counterintuitive to the development of empathy—how can we find common purpose when we are striving to score a win for our side above all else?

This chapter discusses how, with a few tweaks to the way debate is conceptualized and implemented, this practice can position young people as engaged and thoughtful citizens (as opposed to mere citizens-in-training), build relational trust and democratic community within classrooms and across schools, and foster the development of critical civic empathy through mutual humanization and a commitment to civic action. There is an old saying that I like to paraphrase as, "There are three sides to every story—yours, mine, and the truth." If we can reimagine the nature and purpose of debate so that "wins" represent the ability to empathize with perspectives that we ourselves may not personally hold—with the ultimate victory being the equitable shared governance of a multivoiced democracy and pursuit of a shared "truth"—then it becomes yet another tool that teachers can use to (re)construct beloved communities in their classrooms and beyond.

DEBATE IN ACTION:
THE MIDDLE SCHOOL QUALITY INITIATIVE

"Look, you can't win all the time, but you know that I think you're all winners just by being here and putting yourselves out there."

The 24 middle schoolers in the classroom let out a collective "Awwww" as sheepish grins sweep across their faces. Ms. Stratton turns to me and confides, "I'm hard as nails but also very mothering." She turns back to her students, calling, "If they ask you something and you don't know the answer, don't just stand there. Come up with a response and ask another question."

We are not in the middle of an English class—we are at a debate tournament on a chilly Saturday morning in March. These 6th-, 7th-, and 8th-graders from the Bronx are in their assigned preparation room, along with hundreds of other students from across New York City, gearing up for their first round. Today's topic: whether the United States should enact stricter gun regulations.

Students have prepared arguments, both pro and con. Some stand in the corner practicing their speeches, underlining words to emphasize or noting places to pause for dramatic effect. Marisa, the team captain, teaches a first-time debater how to "flow"—debate lingo for taking notes. "Now you have to figure out what you're going to say against that argument," she declares. All of the students are wearing bright red T-shirts emblazoned with their school name; on the back, the shirts read, "What's your evidence? Because I strongly disagree. #Debaters."

Raymond—a tall, skinny 7th-grader—races around the room hugging his fellow team members. He runs up to Ms. Stratton and exclaims, "I'm scared of this topic!" She gives him a reassuring hug and tells him to keep preparing.

She turns back to me with a gentle smile. "Debate builds relationships. I get to see them growing up."

Fast forward to the third and final round of the day. Raymond and his partner, Jared, are arguing the "con" side, working hard to cast doubt on the effectiveness of regulations at reducing gun violence. The duo cited evidence that despite increased gun control measures in Chicago, crime continues unabated. Their opponents insisted that without regulations, the situation would be even worse. But Jared persisted, declaring, "Stricter regulations do not correlate to a reduction in violent crime. Criminals will still get guns regardless of regulations. The people who will be hurt are those who want to own firearms legally for protection." As the evidence-based argument continued, the volunteer judge furiously jotted down notes. When the round ended, Raymond and Jared immediately dropped their serious demeanor—they grinned and shook hands with their opponents before running excitedly to the auditorium to await the awards ceremony.

I wrote this vignette after spending a day at a debate tournament organized by the Middle School Quality Initiative (MSQI), a program affiliated with the New York City Department of Education (NYCDOE) and supported by the New York City Council. Since 2013, MSQI has worked with a growing number of public middle schools across the city (now up to 130 schools) to implement standards-based reading practices in classrooms across content areas and foster schoolwide commitments to literacy. The goal of the program is to ensure that as many 8th-graders as possible leave middle school reading on or above grade level so as to put them on a pathway for success in high school, college, and beyond.

I became connected to MSQI as a result of my own experiences as a debate coach when I taught English at a New York City high school at the beginning of my career. During my first year of teaching, my classroom was right next door to the room of Ben Honoroff, a veteran history teacher at the school. Ben quickly became a mentor who guided me through the trials and tribulations of new teacher-hood, and in the process, he recruited me to assist him with managing the policy debate team that he coached after school. From that point on, Ben and I taught nearly 40 students per year the intricacies of policy debate, a format in which students propose (or refute) policy solutions to intractable challenges facing the United States—recent topics have included education reform, diplomatic relations with China, and domestic surveillance. Our team achieved a great deal of success in the New York City Urban Debate League (NYCUDL), the largest member of the National Association of Urban Debate Leagues (NAUDL), an organization focused on providing young people in city schools opportunities and support to excel at this literacy-rich activity.

Years later, as I completed my graduate work, Ben joined the staff of MSQI and coached several schools through the implementation of Word Generation, a curriculum developed by Harvard researcher Catherine Snow and the Strategic Education Research Partnership (SERP), geared toward increasing students' reading comprehension levels through academic language instruction and classroom discussions across disciplines. The curriculum features vocabulary-rich interdisciplinary units that culminate in high-interest weekly debates about current social issues (even if your school does not use the Word Generation curriculum, free resources are available for download at wordgen.serpmedia.org/).

Recalling the benefits that students from our previous school reaped from participating in the NYCUDL, Ben proposed organizing an MSQI debate program in which students could bring their Word Generation classroom debates out into the community and across the MSQI network. MSQI began sponsoring four tournaments throughout the school year in which students debated popular topics from the Word Generation curriculum—tournaments that now attract hundreds of students apiece.

Ben told me about this new iteration of debate and the desire of the MSQI team to learn more about what they already viscerally understood—that this activity was having transformative effects not only on the students who participated, but also on their teachers, administrators, and entire school communities. I came on board to help document these positive benefits. I knew that academic research had already established some of ways that classroom discussion could impact students, including potential improvements in reading comprehension and vocabulary development (Applebee, Langer, Nystrand, & Gamoran, 2003; Snow, Lawrence, & White, 2009) and commitments to critical thinking and civic participation (Hess & McAvoy, 2014).

I began my research by exploring how students in the program responded to debate and slowly expanded my focus outward to include teachers and entire school communities. I found that participation in debate benefited students' academic literacy and critical-thinking skills (findings that both had been discussed in the literature previously), and also their dispositions toward critical consciousness and civic engagement. I briefly discuss each of these findings below and explain the link between debate and critical civic empathy. I then turn to the story of one particular school to illustrate how educators can begin to think about possibilities for debate in their own contexts.

ACADEMIC AND CIVIC BENEFITS OF DEBATE

To better understand the reading, writing, listening, and speaking skills necessary to engage in debate, let's consider the format of one MSQI debate round. I first should note that many different kinds of debate exist, each with its own structure and style. MSQI debates utilize the public format structure (with some modifications made for middle school students). In this format, the debate is built around a resolution; in the case of the round discussed in the vignette above, the resolution was: Resolved: The United States should enact stricter gun regulations. The pro team is tasked with supporting this resolution; the con team, with refuting it (each team has two members). The round proceeds through a series of timed speeches punctuated by "crossfires," or question-and-answer sessions used to clarify and critique opponents' arguments (see Figure 2.1).

During the first two rounds of speeches, debaters construct their arguments and offer evidence to support them. In the summary and final focus speeches, debaters cannot offer new arguments, only evidence to support the arguments that have already been made. The judge is responsible for awarding the win to the team that offers the most compelling and best supported arguments *and* refutes each of the opposing team's arguments. Taking notes—or "flowing"—is key to success in a round in order to ensure that all arguments are addressed, since a "dropped" argument could make all the difference between a win and a loss. Similarly, research is a core element of debate because the sources from which evidence is drawn can become key points of contention during a round.

The skills associated with debate align with the literacy standards that guide classroom instruction. For instance, the Common Core State Standards highlight the need for students to be able to craft arguments that harness evidence in support of reasonable and persuasive claims—a practice that is at the heart of debate. When I interviewed 24 student debaters, six teacher coaches, and four administrators from four focus MSQI schools about the effects of debate on their lives, every single student confirmed that participation in debate bolstered his or her argumentation skills. Simone, a 7th-grade debater from Polaris Academy in Brooklyn, explained how as a result of debate she learned to consider counterarguments each time she approached a new text: "We were reading the passage as a class and every single contention, every single reason that [the author] had as to why this was right, I'd automatically think in my head why this was wrong. Or if [the author] had why it was wrong, I'd automatically think of why it was right. So, it kind of—after a while, it does become second nature to us."

Literacy standards also call for students to learn how to evaluate information for accuracy and credibility. Alexander, an 8th-grade debater from Eastside Community Middle School in Queens, shared how participation in debate made him more discerning when choosing sources for essays in class:

Figure 2.1. MSQI Public Forum Debate Format

Speeches	Time Limits
Speaker 1 (Team A, 1st speaker)	4 minutes
Speaker 2 (Team B, 1st speaker)	4 minutes
Crossfire (between speakers 1 & 2)	3 minutes
Speaker 3 (Team A, 2nd speaker)	4 minutes
Speaker 4 (Team B, 2nd speaker)	4 minutes
Crossfire (between speakers 3 & 4)	3 minutes
Speaker 1 Summary	2 minutes
Speaker 2 Summary	2 minutes
Grand Crossfire (all speakers)	3 minutes
Speaker 3 Final Focus	2 minutes
Speaker 4 Final Focus	2 minutes

Note: Each team may use up to 2 minutes of prep time.

"Debate taught me how to research things well, because when I used to research topics for school, I just looked at what popped up first on Google and I'm like, 'Okay, that's it.' But now you have to make sure the sources are reliable and everything. You can't just go on Wikipedia and stuff." Alexander's quote demonstrates not only how debate reinforces the practice of evidence-based writing, but also how it promotes critical media literacy—the very skill that protects citizens from being manipulated by misleading rhetoric or baldly false information.

In addition to interviewing students and adults involved in debate about its academic literacy benefits, I also worked with the MSQI team to analyze participating students' standardized reading comprehension test scores. While a full discussion of the analysis is beyond the scope of this chapter (you can read more about it in Mirra, Honoroff, Elgendy, & Pietrzak, 2016), we found that debaters experienced statistically significant greater growth in reading comprehension skills than peers who did not debate, when controlling for race, ability, income, language, and baseline test scores. These findings are consistent with the aforementioned research on the reading comprehension and vocabulary development benefits of debate.

These academic effects are crucial in their own right; indeed, independent evaluations commissioned by Urban Debate Leagues across the country demonstrate that debate can help combat academic opportunity gaps faced by students of color and low-income students in city schools (Houston Independent School District, 2012; Minneapolis Public Schools, 2015).

Nonetheless, I was even more interested in considering the effects of debate on students' civic competencies; debate is central to public deliberation at every level of governance and it is important that young people from historically minoritized communities are able to leverage the full rights of citizenship (Cridland-Hughes, 2012).

Considering that each debate resolution focuses on a topic related to current events, it is not surprising that debate helps increase students' civic knowledge. Amaya, a 6th-grade debater from Eastside Community Middle School, told me, "I did not look at current events before debate. But recently when I went to my grandparents' house, I watched the news a lot and it was interesting to me. Current events are always exciting, but before I didn't have my eyes open to it." Mr. Lizzio, a teacher at Ripken Middle School, shared, "I don't know too many 6th-grade students who would talk about nuclear power during lunchtime. Now, I mean, they're definitely more in-tune to current events and what's going on in the world."

And more than simply helping students become aware of current events, debate aids students in recognizing multiple perspectives about those events because they have to be prepared to argue both for and against resolutions—even when one side might conflict with their personal beliefs. Anna, a 7th-grade debater from Polaris Academy, described how the perspective-taking inherent to debate can foster understanding between individuals with different life experiences or beliefs: "When you have a different point of view, you know how to approach everything differently. So, you know how to adapt to more people." A willingness to listen and adapt to various social situations is crucial for empathy because of the respect it affords individuals with differing opinions and the commitment it offers to the development of shared solutions to common challenges.

Importantly, however, this understanding of multiple perspectives does not imply that students succumb to moral relativism and believe that every perspective is equally valid; instead, through the careful teaching of their coaches about how strong arguments are constructed and how to assess the validity and rigor of every claim's intellectual foundations, debaters become more sophisticated about recognizing bias and questioning faulty assumptions—both their own and those of others. This competency follows them out of the classroom and into today's contentious social context. For example, Anthony, an 8th-grade debater from Glory Academy in the Bronx, explained how debate helped him process and formulate responses to the recent news about officer-involved shootings of Black men: "I can use [debate] toward life, because now I will be there as a reminder when it comes to things like the Eric Garner case and the Michael Brown case. Now I understand both sides. Even though I stand strong to one side, I understand where the other side is coming from." Understanding the viewpoints of those who did not see racism at work in these incidents helped him to better buttress his own analysis and construct arguments that could effectively challenge color-blind perspectives. This is where the critical and civic aspects of empathy emerge as young people consider the issues of power at play in public dialogue.

Indeed, because the MSQI debate program is dedicated to opening the world of debate to young people historically excluded from formalized extracurricular programs and to insisting that their voices matter in both school and society, students emerge from the debating experience with commitments to engaging in social action and standing up against injustice. Kara, a 7th-grade debater from Eastside Community Middle School, told me, "Debate really brought me out and into the world, and it exposed me—that's why I love doing debate. Because I can show what I'm feeling, and not just keep it inside to myself, and stand up for people and their rights." Anna from Polaris Academy added, "I'm just like, wow. This is the world we live in. I can do something to help, even if it's like a little thing. Like I said, I like writing. I can do something to reach out to people. Talk to my peers."

Benjamin, a 6th-grade debater from Glory Academy, captured both the general power that debate holds for all young people and the specific benefits of debate for students of color in city schools when he summed up why this activity mattered to him: "Debate makes me feel like I'm actually good at something that I never thought I would have the chance to do." Benjamin's words sum up the role of debate as a generator of critical civic empathy.

DEBATE AND CRITICAL CIVIC EMPATHY

At its most basic level, debate represents a step in the right direction in terms of treating young people as active citizens by simply encouraging them to *talk*. In many classrooms, particularly those that serve high proportions of students from minoritized communities, teachers do the lion's share of the talking in class (Lingard, Hayes, & Mills, 2003). And when students do talk, their contributions often are limited to answering teachers' questions (Cazden, 2001). True dialogue between young people is the foundation not only of academic learning, but of democratic life itself; no one made this connection more forcefully than American educational philosopher John Dewey.

What makes Dewey's (1916) views on dialogue so unique and crucial to this project is that he does not view communication as the means to an end (such as achieving democracy), but the end in itself—as he describes, "Society not only continues to exist *by* transmission, *by* communication, but it may fairly be said to exist *in* transmission, *in* communication" (p. 5, emphasis original). In other words, communication is not a precondition for democracy—the process embodies democracy itself. Dewey argues that "democracy is more than a form of government; it is primarily a mode of associated living, of conjoint communicated experience" (p. 101). Dialogue defines democracy for Dewey because he sees the communicative process as the source of all knowledge, meaning, and identity—the essence of shared collective life. For him, knowledge does not exist independently, but is created through dialogue between individuals.

So, does this mean that any form of debate in the classroom is a step toward the development of critical civic empathy? Not quite. While some might contend that debate, regardless of its conceptualization or implementation, fosters empathy simply because it encourages students to consider opposing perspectives on controversial issues, I suggest that this argument is flawed, largely because it flattens the issues of power, positionality, and historicity that are at play in any intellectual exchange of ideas. If we as teachers integrate debates into our classrooms without considering these issues, we risk facilitating empty academic exercises that can fail to achieve or even actively counter the aims of critical civic empathy.

This consideration is particularly important in today's political moment in which teachers increasingly are being called upon to help young people process controversies that are dominating the national media conversation. From the NFL #TakeAKnee protests to the White supremacist marches in Charlottesville, Virginia, to the devastatingly common recent school shootings, articles have been popping up in major media outlets after each new event about how teachers should talk to their students about them. Considering the fear that many educators possess about appearing to support partisan political positions in their teaching (Journell, 2016), it may seem wisest to use debate to approach these issues in order to allow for a multiplicity of perspectives and avoid the danger of bias. We cannot be accused of supporting one side if we simply assign students randomly to perspectives and argue it out, right?

It's not so easy. Every pedagogical choice we make has implications about what we value and want our students to value, what matters and what does not; in short, every choice teachers make is political (Nieto, 2006)— not necessarily partisan, but political nonetheless. Of course, there is never enough time to introduce students to all of the texts and ideas we'd like to, but the nature, purpose, and range of the texts and ideas we do make time for in the classroom invariably send messages to students about the values and principles that we deem most valuable for them to retain as they progress into society. These voices are necessary, while those are not. There is no escaping it—even if we vow to remain objective and avoid talking about any topics other than those outlined in the mandated district curriculum, we are making political choices.

But wait, you might argue—if I am making the choice to integrate current events into my curriculum and using the practice of debate to unearth multiple perspectives, aren't I making a political choice oriented toward empathy? Maybe yes, but maybe no. This is because political perspectives are not always mere differences of opinion on the nature of and approaches to addressing policy issues about which reasonable people might disagree; rather, more and more in today's polarized climate, political perspectives represent deep philosophical beliefs about who belongs in this country and who does not, or who deserves the full rights of humanity and who does not. Foundational, bedrock beliefs about (de)humanization hum just below the surface of debate. While assigning students randomly to debate the pros and cons of nuclear power may not seem to immediately touch upon the intimate facets of our identities and positionality in society, assigning them to debate about immigration or criminal justice or police brutality just might. This realization doesn't mean that we should avoid exploring these issues with our students, but rather that they require much more foresight and care than simply dividing students into teams and letting them have at it.

At the most basic level, we likely can agree that perspectives denigrating or attacking any person or persons on the basis of any identity attributes are not deserving of empathy; however, at a time when it is becoming more and more difficult to separate political positions from judgments of identity (hence the phrase "identity politics"), enforcing even this fundamental rule can become murky. In their book *The Political Classroom*, Diana Hess and Paula McAvoy (2014) discuss the need for teachers to make distinctions between "empirical" and "political" issues and "open" and "settled" issues in their classrooms in order to clarify which topics are permissible and which are off the table for debate. In overly simplistic terms, empirical issues are those that can be answered with evidence, whereas political issues are those in which the choice of an appropriate response has multiple and competing views. Layered on top of this is the idea that some issues are considered open in our society, in that reasonable people continue to disagree on the best course of action, while others are considered settled, in that a consensus about them has been reached in society. Hess and McAvoy use the issue of climate change as an example; they suggest that the question of whether it exists is empirically settled but that what to do about it is politically open. Of course, they then note that in our current political climate, battles over what is empirically proven can reignite when folks use different news sources that confuse or outright misrepresent facts.

Going back to the typology of critical civic empathy, the difference I'm discussing here is between defining political perspectives as individual opinions and defining them as ideologies representative of larger issues of power and identity—and hence, between individual empathy and critical civic empathy. A common characteristic of the partisan sparring taking place on cable news and in political campaigns at the moment is the impulse to immediately respond to an argument by positing a counterargument and demanding that both "sides" have equal merit and must receive equal consideration, even if evidence indicates that the arguments are not equally rigorous. The term that logisticians use to describe this situation is *false equivalence*. Late-night TV host John Oliver comically explored this phenomenon on his show using the issue of climate change, explaining that while 99 out of every 100 scientists agree that climate change is a real and man-made issue—for all intents and purposes representing a consensus—media outlets consistently invite one climate change believer and one climate skeptic onto their shows to debate the issue as if those sides were equivalent. Such debates misrepresent facts and degrade political dialogue to the point where individuals are defending their arguments with phrases like, "Well, that's my opinion," without considering the ideologies they are promulgating, some of which question the worth of communities based on their race, immigration status, gender, sexual orientation, or religious affiliation.

What does this mean for classroom debate? I suggest that if we want to ensure that our classrooms are spaces committed to the development of critical civic empathy, we need to consider the ideologies that circulate in our classrooms and the kinds of dialogue that are permitted and excluded. As teachers, we are tasked with creating safe and welcoming learning environments for all of our students, and most school codes of conduct explicitly forbid discrimination or prejudice. I believe that this applies not only to direct interpersonal interactions between students, but also to the discourses we ask students to consider in class. Consider, for example, a class debate about immigration policy. Without careful planning and explicit teaching about issues of xenophobia and racism, students could be offering nativist arguments in class that could be extremely painful and dangerous for undocumented students with no context other than arguing an assigned side. Debate is not (and should not be) a free-for-all of perspectives, but rather an exchange that has ground rules of humanization.

In order to frame these debates with care, I concentrate on two elements—analyzing the nature and sources of potential evidence and reviewing the bedrock principles of democratic deliberation. To return to the immigration debate as an example, we might analyze the argument that immigration increases crime and find that this claim rests upon anecdotes of individual incidents that have been statistically debunked—this discovery can spur conversations about validity, reliability, and the reason that certain media sites might publish such a claim. We can then decide as a group about the standards we insist upon for evidence in our classrooms. In addition, I talk openly with students about the ideas that are not compatible with democratic life. As researchers Benjamin Justice and Jason Stanley (2016) remind us, "Democratic principles and ideals are not themselves neutral. Neither is teaching students to become citizens in a society that aspires to these ideals" (p. 40).

It is possible to debate controversial issues in ways that first honor the worth of all parties involved; and at the same time, it is appropriate to deem some topics as off limits for debate altogether if they are framed in a way that invites discriminatory argumentation. The coaches and organizers of the MSQI debate program work diligently to ensure that middle school students are treated as civic agents capable of discussing complex social issues but can do so with arguments that do not threaten the humanity of any community. We can do the same thing in our classrooms when we commit ourselves to historicizing issues with our students and exposing the deep-seated beliefs about communities that are at play in seemingly innocuous policy positions.

When we approach debate from a standpoint of collective humanization, we also are addressing the other axis of the critical civic empathy typology—the commitment to social action. Instead of simply using debate as one of a series of discussion formats in order to complete academic exercises, we can take a more in-depth approach that provides a model for democratic deliberation and serves as a catalyst for further civic action in class. As referenced in Chapter 1, classroom discussions can serve as segues for writing to local and national officials. Yet even in and of itself, treating public dialogue as a serious enterprise and striving to foster communication across difference in a way that honors the experiences and voices of diverse participants in our democracy are enactments of critical civic empathy.

So, what does it look like when teachers and entire school communities commit to debate as a catalyst for literacy and civic learning? We turn now to the story of one MSQI school that can inspire you to consider actions you can take in your own classroom context.

DEBATE AT UNIDAD MIDDLE SCHOOL: A CASE STUDY

Remember Ben Honoroff, my friend and colleague who helped start the MSQI debate program? He later became principal of a middle school in Brooklyn and brought his commitment to the transformative power of debate to the task of re-energizing a school struggling to combat low test scores, declining enrollment, and the effects of community gentrification. The work that he and the staff at Unidad Middle School have accomplished speaks to the ways that teachers can use debate to spark dialogue across entire school communities.

Ben explained to me how the MSQI debate program's grounding in the aforementioned Word Generation curriculum—implemented across grade levels and subject areas at all MSQI schools—made it easy to get his entire staff to feel invested in a common goal when he arrived at Unidad:

> So, we used the curriculum as a unifier of practices across disciplines by addressing a high interest debate topic every week in all of the subject areas across the entire school. It was a real culture builder for the staff. I was able to say in one of the first staff meetings that if we come back from this first debate tournament with a trophy, it won't be a victory just for our debate coaches; it will be a victory for the whole school. Because you

know, take the genetic testing debate topic. Math classes were studying the statistics of genetic testing, science classes were studying the science of genetic testing, social studies classes were studying the ethics of genetics testing, and ELA classes were looking at the rhetoric of genetic testing.

Ben also stressed that because all students in the school experienced Word Generation, all students could participate in the MSQI debate program—not just high-achieving students. As he explained, "We have debaters with disabilities, we have debaters who are English language learners, we have debaters from our transitional bilingual class." Indeed, MSQI debate tournaments now include a bilingual division to honor and support all students' linguistic resources.

As the debate team has grown over the years and news of its success has spread throughout the community, Ben and his debate coaches have found parents of elementary school students eager to send their children to Unidad for middle school. The team attends middle school fairs and stages mock debate rounds to demonstrate the activity for younger students. As Ben shares, "Because of that, a lot of families wanted to come to this school. Parents saw students who were highly committed to this academic activity and they saw in those students what their 5th-graders could be."

A typical debate practice at Unidad could be mistaken for a formal English language arts class. On a Thursday in October, 6th-grade ELA teacher Robert Davis is helping students understand the issue that will be the focus of the first tournament of the year: genetic testing. The topic is posted on a piece of chart paper on the classroom wall: "The United States government should regulate genetic testing," along with blank posters labeled "Pro" and "Con" that students will start filling in with ideas.

Mr. Davis projects a scenario onto the screen at the front of the room. It reads:

> Jeff and Susan have always wanted to have a baby. Their doctor said that they could use genetic testing to choose whether they had a boy or a girl. Some people argue that genetic testing should only be used to diagnose and predict medical problems, not to design their babies.
>
> What is your perspective? Support your perspective with two reasons.

The 21 6th-graders in the room immediately begin buzzing with ideas. Mr. Davis asks one young man, "Where do you stand on this?" He replies, "If doctors can design babies, it could get into the wrong hands and they could say that only babies with certain traits could be born and others have to be eliminated." A young woman across the room chimes in, "I want to add on to what he said. I think people shouldn't play God. Let's say you try to get rid of a disease—something worse might appear."

Mr. Davis nods and says that they will be building a "we can't play God" argument for their pro speeches. "But," he challenges the students, "if I was debating against you I would ask, 'What is your evidence for that?'" One student begins to share a story he saw on a TV law drama. "We can't use TV shows!" Mr. Davis exclaims good-naturedly. "Your judge would be going crazy."

He reminds students about the article they read on the topic the day before and tells them that they are going to do an evidence scavenger hunt. He divides students into groups and gives each group an envelope filled with slips of paper containing claims—some true, some false. Students need to evaluate each claim by referring to particular pieces of evidence given in the article. One group chooses a slip of paper that reads, "Patients who carry the BRCA1 gene are guaranteed to get some form of cancer." The students read back through the article and find the quote explaining that the cancer risk for individuals with this gene is 85%, not 100%. They write down on their scavenger hunt sheet why this claim is false.

In an interview after the practice ended, Mr. Davis explained, "Evidence-based argumentation is the focus of this school, so it's a logical next step that our school would be known for debate. That's what debate is all about." He waved a hand across the room where the children had been and said, "All of these students are brand new to debate. And they don't all come in at the highest levels of literacy. We have students with IEPs, students who are learning English. Debate is what draws them in."

Ben reiterated the ways that debate supported Unidad's schoolwide literacy focus:

> It is at the heart of Common Core standards—not just in English but also across subject areas. Argumentation and explanation and use of academic language and being able to evaluate evidence—this is at the heart of everything that we're asking our teachers to do. It's not a gimmicky theme—it's a theme that's at the heart of good education. It's about creating critical thinkers—debate is at the heart of that.

Ben aimed to make sure that his entire student population—including the high percentage of recent immigrant students—could access and benefit from debate. He encouraged students to debate in Spanish as they learned the English language and pushed the MSQI debate program to implement the bilingual division at tournaments to be more inclusive. Students who arrived in the country just weeks prior attended debate tournaments and immediately began competing, thereby creating a pathway to academic and civic life in a new country.

June 9, 2017: the final MSQI debate tournament of the year. Each school can bring only three student teams to compete in the championship competition to tackle the topic: "The United States federal government should abolish solitary confinement in all prisons." Unidad Middle School is the host of this tournament, and as all of the students and coaches gather in the school cafeteria, it is impossible to miss the massive team in their blue T-shirts (Unidad: Pride of the Southside)—they are practically bursting with excitement and pride to have the entire MSQI debate community on their home turf.

The MSQI debate program recognizes the need for students to feel proud of themselves and their schools, which is why, in addition to individual speaker awards, each tournament also features recognition for the schools whose teams rack up the most wins overall. This recognition makes all students feel that they are contributing to the team—even if they win only one round out of three in a day—since these victories are tallied and celebrated.

The powerhouse Unidad team placed first overall at three of the four tournaments during the 2016–2017 school year. These wins were especially meaningful for a school that was losing enrollment and on the brink of closure just a few years prior. Ben described the importance of debate for the students, parents, and teachers of his school:

It's been a prideful thing in the community. I think that any type of competition brings a school together, but especially one that is an intellectual competition with academic rigor. It's something that is very prideful. You know, we've been faced with lots of labels. We were labeled a Renewal school, a State Focus school, and a Persistently Dangerous school. With all of these negative labels, to also be labeled "debate city champion" is something that can counter a lot of the negativity that is foisted upon us.

Civic leaders increasingly are taking note of the ways that debate is empowering the young adults in their districts. The city council has begun a yearly tradition of inviting MSQI debaters to one of their public meetings to engage in a showcase debate on the floor of city hall. The representative for the Unidad community greeted students on the steps of city hall at the latest showcase in early June and told them about the connections between the activity of debate and city leadership. "That's what we do in there," he said, pointing inside the building. "We debate all day." He then met each student's gaze and stated, "Hopefully you'll be here one day."

Ben expanded upon the theme of voice as he considered the benefits to his Unidad students:

For students, I think it honors their voice. It's empowering for a judge to listen solely to them for an hour on a Saturday. And it helps them to become more critical viewers of the media and just understand that their voices matter in these contemporary issues.

The deputy borough president for Brooklyn attended the final MSQI debate tournament of the year to celebrate those student voices. She left the debaters with a powerful reminder about their responsibility to use their voices to better society: "Don't just debate. Take these skills and use them. Create the world we want to see!"

CONCLUSION

The MSQI debate program, and the story of Unidad Middle School in particular, demonstrates how debate can be transformed from a classroom activity into a form of critical community literacy that fosters empathy through commitments to cultivating the civic agency of young people and implementing culturally sustaining practices that support humanization and social justice. Debate does not have to be considered an activity for a small, specialized group of students, but instead can be designed as a galvanizing force for young people across schools and districts that encourages them to raise their voices, speak their opinions, and value themselves as citizens as well as scholars. Parents, teachers, and administrators are clamoring for schools to prepare young people to lead 21st-century civic life in a more compassionate and collaborative direction. Debate has the potential to answer that charge for a new generation of citizens.

Although the development of a league like MSQI takes time and coordination, there are many small moves that English teachers can make to begin thinking about debate differently in their classrooms. You can consider the themes and controversies that are embedded explicitly or implicitly in the texts that you read with your students and design debates around those issues. You can coordinate with members of subject or grade-level teams to pinpoint topics for debate that might engage material from multiple content areas. And you can partner with parents, community members, and local elected officials to offer students the opportunity to dialogue before authentic "judges."

One of the first activities that I do whenever I'm introducing students to debate is teach them how to flow—that, again, is debate lingo for note-taking. Flowing is crucial when arguments are coming at a debater left and right because failing to respond to any claim during a debate (or "dropping" it) is a sure way to lose a round. A simple way to introduce flowing is to fold a piece of paper until you have four columns and six rows (a template can be found in Appendix B). I then introduce a silly resolution that requires little prior knowledge, such as: Dogs are better pets than cats. I choose pairs of students to argue the pro and con sides while other students practice flowing on the board or at their seats. Each team comes up with three arguments for its position and engages in 3-minute rounds in which students support their points and refute those of the other team. Hilarity often ensues at the ridiculous claims being made, and students enjoy comparing the number of arguments they captured on their flow sheet. Once students have been hooked, I am able to demonstrate how the tactics we used in jest to argue a largely inconsequential issue bear striking similarities to those employed by political candidates to contest issues of much deeper import. While we might have laughed when attempting to characterize all felines as devious and evil, we suddenly can see the deadly serious consequences of essentializing rhetoric when used to discuss immigrants. At this point, students are ready to delve into significant civic issues.

On a deeper level, sustained inquiry into the nature and purpose of debate reminds us of the importance of language as a mediator of our worlds—the ones we live in as well as the ones we hope to create. When we step back and consider the language we as teachers use toward our students and the language we encourage our students to use with one another, we realize that we are creating tiny microcosms of democratic life in each of our classrooms. We are showing students possibilities of how we can live together in diverse societies—in strife or in solidarity—and the vulnerability and care that it takes to truly strive to understand those with whom we differ in fundamental ways.

DISCUSSION/REFLECTION QUESTIONS

1. What experiences (if any) have you had with implementing discussions and debates about current events in your classroom? What kinds of discourses circulate among students and how do you handle them?

2. Consider a controversial social issue that relates to your curriculum. How could you go about historicizing this issue with your students in order to create the foundation for more empathetic debate?

3. What norms and structures need to be in place for your students to have humanizing and compassionate dialogue? How could you go about developing these?

4. What opportunities might exist for you to partner with colleagues or community members to bring debate from the classroom to the community?

CHAPTER 3

Who Gets to Produce Knowledge?

Harnessing Youth Expertise Through Participatory Action Research

In their landmark study of 20th-century public school reform efforts, educational historians David Tyack and Larry Cuban (1995) discovered a paradox—despite massive social, economic, and technological shifts, the structures and practices of schools remained largely static. And this continuity stretches into our current context; for the most part, a 9th-grader from the 1920s could time travel into a school today and recognize much of what she would see in terms of the subject areas, bell schedules, and even many instructional strategies. Tyack and Cuban capture this persistent way of doing things with a phrase that English teachers can appreciate—they call it the "grammar of schooling" (p. 85).

I am taken by this phrase because it captures the sense of tradition that often can constrain us as educators. Just as we assume that sentences must be constructed according to prescriptive rules, so do we assume that particular activities must be assigned in order to make a class a "proper" representative of its subject. For English teachers, one activity that serves as a rite of passage is the research paper.

I can recall clearly my first experience with the literary analysis research paper in high school—crafting a thesis statement, discovering primary and secondary sources, and mining quotes to buttress my argument. I also remember the rules that governed each of these steps. The thesis statement had to have three parts. The secondary sources had to come from reputable approved outlets. Evidence had to come from experts. And for heaven's sake, the first-person voice had to be avoided at all costs.

In hindsight, I can see that I never felt any authority during this process. I considered my opinions valuable only to the extent that they were confirmed by *real* researchers. I organized existing knowledge into a coherent text but did not believe for a second that I was contributing any new ideas to the world. It was an exercise in imitation. And while there certainly is value in developing skills through mimicry, I believe now that something crucial about the research endeavor is missing when the researcher is divorced from the experience of actually producing and disseminating new knowledge.

The assumption that guides the traditional research paper activity in schools is that young people do not possess expertise in any subject. The purpose of their research efforts is simply to learn the rules of the game so that one day, if they so choose, they can earn the proper credentials needed to make definitive proclamations of knowledge. Although crafted with good intentions, the underlying message that we give students when we tell them that they can't use the "I" pronoun in research writing, or that a thought is valid only when it is published by an academic press, is that respected truth comes from outside sources—not from them or their communities.

My stance on research transformed when I learned about a practice called youth participatory action research (YPAR). YPAR interrogates normative views about what research is, who can engage in it, and what its purposes are in society, all in pursuit of a more expansive and equitable concept of expertise. Proponents of YPAR contend that research should be considered rigorous and influential only to the extent that it honors multiple perspectives and is conducted in a democratic manner aimed at addressing challenges meaningful to the communities involved.

While we soon will explore the ways that YPAR engages with ideas about truth and knowledge reaching all the way back to the Enlightenment era, for now let me offer a starting definition. YPAR is the practice of encouraging young people to develop their own research questions about topics that are meaningful to them and related to issues or challenges they see reflected in their communities. They then gather data about these topics in a variety of ways that leverage the knowledge of local experts and personal experience. YPAR gained increased attention with the publication of two seminal texts in 2008: Julio Cammarota and Michelle Fine's *Revolutionizing Education* and Jeff Duncan-Andrade and Ernest Morrell's *The Art of Critical Pedagogy*. Both texts explore the long history of participatory action research (PAR) as a method to amplify the perspectives of minoritized communities in social science and public health research, as well as the conscious decision to add the "Y" in order to privilege the often-overlooked expertise of youth. YPAR has grown in popularity in the years since, with more school-based educators interested in facilitating a process that was once more the province of after-school and community educators. The YPAR Hub, developed by Emily Ozer at the University of California, Berkeley, serves as a repository of information about YPAR programs around the world (yparhub.berkeley.edu/).

In this chapter, I present ideas about how to use YPAR to transform research writing in the English classroom by drawing on my experiences engaging in the practice both inside and outside of schools. I argue that YPAR has the potential to foster critical civic empathy in several ways, the most transformative of which is its ability to help young people see their own thoughts, experiences, and voices as valued sources of knowledge. It also encourages young people to develop research questions that are relevant to and engaged with authentic civic issues, and explodes traditional forms of data collection, analysis, and presentation by introducing oral history, multimodal composing, and community cultural wealth into the inquiry process. YPAR is a literacy-rich activity that can help us disrupt the grammar of schooling by reimagining not only what expertise our students possess but also what the very purpose of education and inquiry should be in a democratic society.

YOUTH PARTICIPATORY ACTION RESEARCH IN ACTION: PURPOSE, PRACTICE, AND POSITIONING

Take a moment to study this group of PowerPoint slides (see Figures 3.1–3.4). They were created by students from Crockett High School in Los Angeles as part of a presentation to local civic leaders about the quality of education that all California students deserve. The presentation focused on the need for a social and physical school environment characterized by authentic care.

Even without further context about the rationale behind this research, these slides demonstrate the sophisticated use of literacy skills to construct a powerful argument. After the first slide offers a claim, the following slides present three pieces of supporting evidence—data from a survey that students wrote and distributed to students across their school district, a video clip from an interview that they conducted with a Crockett teacher, and theoretical analysis about the nature of oppression (keep in mind that this is a PowerPoint, so the students verbalized most of their reasoning). I don't know a single teacher who wouldn't be thrilled to see students exhibiting this level of literacy skill. And we haven't even scratched the surface in terms

Figure 3.1. YPAR Claim Slide

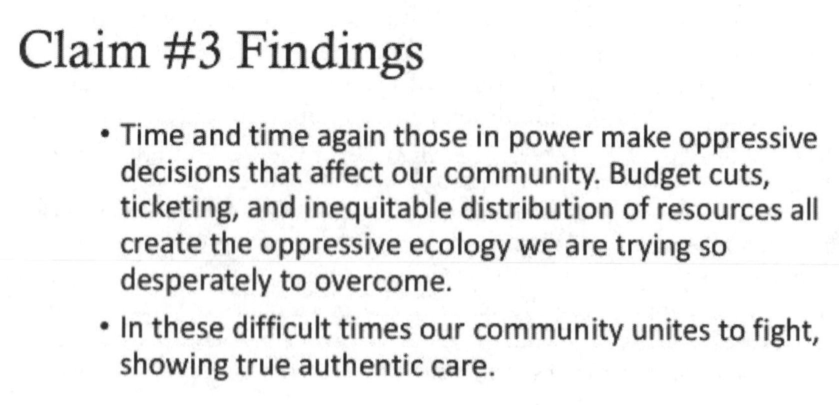

Claim #3 Findings

- Time and time again those in power make oppressive decisions that affect our community. Budget cuts, ticketing, and inequitable distribution of resources all create the oppressive ecology we are trying so desperately to overcome.

- In these difficult times our community unites to fight, showing true authentic care.

Figure 3.2. YPAR Survey Slide

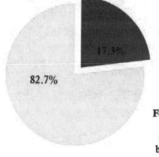

SURVEY QUESTION

My school offers special academic programs and afterschool activities

- Strongly Disagree/ Disagree
- Strongly Agree/ Agree

17.3%

82.7%

Food, health, and academic opportunities dictate our choices. Some of our opportunities are limited and we make better choices when better opportunities are available to us.

Figure 3.3. YPAR Interview Slide

DATA/EVIDENCE

Who is caring?

of the multimodal competencies involved in creating pie charts and embedding video clips into text.

What takes this writing to the next level and moves it from research to YPAR can be summed up as the three Ps: purpose, practice, and positioning. First, the *purpose*. Students decided to explore their research topic—the education that California students deserve—10 years after the filing of a case in California's Supreme Court in which the state found that all students in

Figure 3.4. YPAR Analysis Slide

Oppression

1.People have not discovered their own "superpower".

- "The fear of freedom is greater still in professionals who have not yet discovered for themselves the invasive nature of their action, and who are told that their action is dehumanizing." Freire, Pedagogy of the Oppressed pg.46

2.The oppressive ways our community is framed creates deficit thinking in both the oppressor and the oppressed.

- "The current movements of rebellion, specially those of youth, . . . necessarily reflect the peculiarities of their respective settings..." –Freire, Pedagogy of the Oppressed pg. 1

3.This has an impact on the social and physical ecology of our environment.

California deserved (but did not enjoy) equitable access to a high-quality education. When students learned about this case, they wondered: What exactly constitutes a high-quality education? And 10 years after this court case was filed, are we getting one? As part of a larger group that included students from four other local high schools, they identified what they considered to be the most meaningful elements of a high-quality education and then split them up, taking the lead on exploring one—a caring physical and social environment (the other elements included critical teaching, culturally relevant curriculum, organic leadership, and sufficient resources).

Another event that hit even closer to home also contributed to the students' purpose. Just a few months before their research began, the film *Waiting for Superman* was released. This documentary followed five students from across the country as they navigated the struggling public school system, implying through its title that these students were waiting for superheroes (in the form of education reformers) to save them from their schools and communities. One of the students followed in the documentary attended a middle school that fed into Crockett High School. The film compiled statistics about Crockett's struggles and dubbed it a "dropout factory" that should be avoided at all costs.

Though Crockett students understood all too well the struggles facing their school, they chafed at the flippant way in which the film passed judgment on it. The filmmakers did not acknowledge the generations of community members and activists who dedicated their lives to improving Crockett. The filmmakers did not acknowledge how important Crockett was to the neighborhood's identity. And the filmmakers did not acknowledge that maybe the community had something to say about what was going wrong—and right—at the school. As a result, the students conceptualized their research as an opportunity to speak back to the deficit narrative constructed about their school and name themselves and their fellow community members as the real superheroes.

The students quickly realized that in order to achieve their purpose of challenging the narrative created by conventional researchers, they could not simply rely on the same methods that those researchers used. They needed to develop an alternative form of research *practice*. In doing so, they did not ignore or devalue data from traditional sources—indeed, they pored over district and state reports, statistics, and news stories—but they did recognize that the voices of those being studied were often minimized and set out to capture their stories. Instead of relying only on existing data sets, they learned how to develop their own valid and reliable survey items, coordinated with school leaders to distribute their survey to students across Los Angeles, and analyzed the results for emergent themes. Instead of interviewing only traditional district leaders, they spoke with students, parents, and teachers in their own community about their views. And instead of relying solely on data from others, they mined their own schooling experiences to create oral histories about power and powerlessness in their community.

The merging of purpose and practice in their research also meant that students had to reconsider the medium and audience for their work. Instead of simply producing written reports of their own, they wanted to personally share collaborative, dynamic, multimedia presentations with a wide spectrum of stakeholders, from policymakers and politicians, to administrators and teachers, to family and friends, in order to call for change. They wanted to look into the eyes of adults and make it impossible for those adults to deny the rigor and righteousness of their research. They spoke to scholars at formal educational conferences and to parents at community venues. And they knew how to code-switch in order to persuade multiple audiences.

Embodied within the purpose and practice of this research approach is the *positioning* of young people as experts of their own lived experience and as credible producers of knowledge—the crucial "Y" of YPAR. I use the word *positioning* because it highlights not only the fact that young people are stepping up into positions of authority, but also the reality that adults have a role to play in supporting them along the way. I worked with these students from Crockett, and dozens of other Los Angeles high school students, through the Council of Youth Research, a YPAR collaborative started by UCLA professors Ernest Morrell and John Rogers that sought to amplify the voices of young people about solutions to the most pressing issues facing their schools and communities. Morrell and Rogers got the idea for the council when they realized that students were better positioned than they themselves were as professors to advise administrators looking for help with intractable challenges in district schools.

I joined the council during my graduate studies at UCLA. When I first began coordinating this after-school program (more on the differences between doing YPAR in classrooms versus after-school spaces soon), I thought that a true commitment to YPAR involved giving young people free rein to explore their interests. After all, wouldn't adult input constitute interference and stifle youth voice? What I soon learned is that YPAR does not require the complete abnegation of adult involvement but rather entails a renegotiation of the adult role. Simply sending students off on their own to figure out a form of research that positions them far differently from anything they may have experienced before in their educational lives amounts to setting them up for failure. Educators are needed to introduce and explain YPAR and to set up opportunities that prepare their students to succeed.

But there is a fine line between support and control that practitioners of YPAR are always attempting to navigate. In the council, we sought to construct an umbrella of research topics and resources under which students had the freedom to determine their own paths of inquiry. Constructing this umbrella ensured that we had the capacity to put students in touch with individuals they could interview or to set up visits to locations that would further their data collection. But all of us educators who worked with the council were pushed far out of our comfort zones in becoming facilitators rather than controllers of the learning experience, and in listening to what students needed from us rather than dictating it. While this meant that we sometimes had to watch students take paths that would lead to dead ends in the course of their research, it ultimately led to the development of transformative student agency and truly youth-led knowledge production.

Positioning students as knowledge producers necessarily involves positioning ourselves as learners. In doing so, YPAR takes us full circle back to the purpose of our work and what constitutes success. YPAR does not fit into an educational model in which the goal is for teachers to endow students with knowledge—it works only if the goal is to support the development of confident and inquisitive civic leaders prepared with the skills to tackle challenges we've known for years and challenges we cannot yet imagine. Importantly, this development is not always accompanied by concrete wins along the way. Returning to the Crockett students, their research did not result in an apologetic call from the producers of *Waiting for Superman*. It did not magically lead to drastic changes in the school's test scores. And that was okay because we had discussed with them the often-halting pace of change and the beauty in the struggle toward social justice. We had taken the time to instill in them the idea that their YPAR journeys represented success on its own terms regardless of any other outcome—an impact that would extend outward to affect all who heard and really listened to their presentation.

And indeed, years after the research was conducted, the students' wins are rolling in. Two members of that Crockett group earned teaching credentials and have returned to their community as educators. Another works for a local nonprofit advocating for educational justice. Their teacher implements YPAR into a special class during the school day geared toward supporting young Latino men as leaders.

Let's delve a bit further into the ways that YPAR transforms how we (and our students) think about knowledge production—and how these shifts contribute to the development of critical civic empathy—before going deeper into what it takes to integrate YPAR into classroom instruction.

YOUTH PARTICIPATORY ACTION RESEARCH AND CRITICAL CIVIC EMPATHY

Though an in-depth exploration of the theoretical framework informing YPAR is beyond the scope of this chapter (for more on that check out Mirra, Garcia, & Morrell, 2015), I believe we can be well served by stepping back and considering how this practice challenges traditional perspectives of two concepts: research and youth.

The word *research*, which dates to the late 16th century, comes from the Middle French word *recerche*, which means "to go about seeking." It generally is understood that what is being sought in research is knowledge, understanding, or discovery; in essence, truth. More complicated is the question: Where does truth come from? Within a few decades of the origin of the term *research*, a consensus had emerged that truth emerged largely from scientific inquiry. Enlightenment philosophers helped construct ideas about the production of knowledge that have achieved the level of dogma today, including the rigorous use of hypotheses and experimentation to reveal universal principles about our world and the necessity of seeking objective information from that world rather than from within ourselves.

Although these ideas ushered in the scientific innovations of the Industrial Revolution and broke the hold of religion (Christianity in particular) on Western society's conceptualization of truth, they also served to position a small segment of the population as the ultimate arbiters of knowledge. Consider the quote often attributed to Winston Churchill that "history is written by the victors." Research couched in the language of science has been harnessed throughout history by those in power (read: White cis-gender, heterosexual men) to protect and extend that power, whether through studies claiming the genetic inferiority of African Americans or designating homosexuality an "illness." To tweak Karl Marx's words, those who control the means of knowledge production can exert a great deal of control over society.

By the mid-20th century, as the world saw the narrative of forward scientific progress barrel toward the specter of global world war and potential nuclear annihilation, scholars (led by the philosophers of the Frankfurt School, discussed in the Introduction) began to question ideas of objectivity and neutrality in research. They argued that what is considered factual and normal often represents the interests of those who benefit most from existing social arrangements and that it is impossible to gather knowledge from the world without it being filtered through the consciousness of the observer. Their insistence on a critical examination of whose narratives get to count as truth, has spawned decades of critical theory and the proliferation of viewpoints from historically marginalized perspectives (e.g., feminism, critical race theory, postcolonialism, and more) (Morrell, 2008).

These ideas, though they may seem abstract, have been at the heart of the past century of social justice movements, from the civil rights struggles of the 1960s to the Black Lives Matter and DREAMer campaigns today. Undergirding all of these movements' concrete demands for change lay the imperative to tell truths about society from nondominant perspectives—to disrupt normative ideas about a country that often promotes narratives of meritocracy and equality but simultaneously maintains systems of structural inequity that disproportionately harm minoritized communities. When the young activists leading Black Lives Matter demand that we know and say the names of Black men and women who have fallen victim to police brutality, they are demanding dignity and voice for their narratives and their lives.

In a similar vein, young people who engage in YPAR are demanding dignity and voice for themselves and their communities as expert producers and disseminators of knowledge. These demands are not simply semantic—they serve as clarion calls about the ways that we as teachers should conceptualize and educate the students in our classrooms. Critical educational scholars have been issuing these calls for decades. Luis Moll and his colleagues from the University of Arizona (Moll, Amanti, Neff, & Gonzalez, 1992) developed the concept of "funds of knowledge" to describe the linguistic and cultural resources that young Mexican American students bring to school—a task that they found necessary in order to counter the deficit orientations that teachers often ascribed to those students. Tara Yosso (2006) developed the concept of "community cultural wealth" to describe the assets of nondominant communities—including resilience, aspirations, and the ability to navigate multiple contexts—and counter the idea that a shortage of financial capital implies a lack of other important social values. Instead of seeking to minimize or erase the cultural capital of our students, Django Paris and H. Samy Alim (2017) encourage the development of "culturally sustaining pedagogies" that honor and seek to foster the cultural wealth of nondominant communities.

The recognition that YPAR fosters among students that they, their families, and their neighborhoods possess unique wells of wisdom that they can share with the world, represents not only a form of culturally sustaining pedagogy, but also a source of critical civic empathy. At first, the idea that YPAR could foster empathy may seem a bit counterintuitive; after all, isn't empathy about looking outward to connecting with others instead of looking for value within, as YPAR seems to suggest? I counter that YPAR does indeed support the development of empathy, both for the students who engage in it and for those who witness the results of the students' research, precisely because it reorients our ideas about who can speak truth, the forms that truth can take, and how those truths can help us imagine a more just and equitable democracy.

Let's start with the young people who engage in YPAR. When asked at the end of each school year how they felt they had been impacted by the process of conducting research, the students in the council consistently expressed pride and amazement at capabilities they exhibited that they never before thought they possessed. Erica, one of the Crockett students, explained, "It's important for us to do the research so it's not only other people who are telling our story." Another council student, Carlos, shared, "I never thought I could be such a revolutionary. Doing this tells me that I am not someone who will sit around and take oppression; I am someone who will be an advocate for change."

These comments illustrate the two axes of the empathy typology. Erica's words remind us of the connection between storytelling and humanization—we cannot fully realize our dignity and worth if we are not permitted to tell our own stories. YPAR allowed Erica the opportunity to claim her humanity and offer a counter-narrative to those who would seek to characterize her school and community from a narrow deficit perspective. And Carlos's words demonstrate how YPAR is a form of critical civic action because it orients research toward the purpose of making education and society more equitable rather than simply toward producing knowledge for its own sake. Carlos connected the process of developing and researching questions that were meaningful to him to making change to combat oppression.

YPAR represents a pedagogical enactment of the three major aspects of critical civic empathy for the young people involved. First, it encourages them to consider their positions in society first as young people and second as young people of color living in low-income communities. Next, it enables them to recognize how these social positions lead some to assume that they have nothing to contribute to conversations around knowledge production and social action. And finally, it prepares them to counter these assumptions by using their own experiences and the experiences of their communities to bring new information into the world. In a sense, the students are learning to empathize with the researchers and truth-tellers within themselves that they previously had been taught were nonexistent or unworthy of public celebration.

Of course, YPAR also promotes the development of critical civic empathy in those who experience students' research, from the educators who facilitate the process to the peers and adults who listen to the presentations. The very nature of YPAR invites all who consume or teach about research to interrogate their assumptions of what counts as rigorous data, who gathers the data, and what purposes they serve in schools and society. YPAR educates us about the communities we live and teach in—what our neighbors are concerned about, what they have experienced, and what they need in order to reach their fullest potential in our shared society. It pushes us to consider the truths that can emerge from community-based forms of inquiry. These can include oral histories that capture the lived experiences of local elders as well as more digitally engaged practices like photovoice (de los Rios, 2017), in which stories are told through the curation of photographs taken by local residents. And it challenges us to think about what we are going to do with the information we've gained, once our consciousness has been expanded, in order to address the challenges raised by our fellow citizens.

But wait, there's a catch. For as transformative as YPAR can be, it also requires a great deal of energy and resources, both material and psychological. In order to conduct their research, council students needed cameras and voice recorders. They needed help making contact and setting up appointments with interviewees. They needed transportation to various field sites. And this does not even begin to address the time and effort the guiding teachers needed in order to navigate the changes they would have to make in their practice to support this style of pedagogy, or that the students needed to work through the stereotypes they had internalized about themselves and their communities and to take on identities as researchers. As mentioned earlier, the council was an after-school program and was sponsored by a university, which meant both that it was free from many of the constraints that teachers experience in the classroom and that it benefited from a wealth of resources, including professors who could write grants to obtain funding and graduate students who could earn their way through doctoral programs by dedicating themselves to this program.

What does it take to integrate YPAR into a high school English classroom? What tensions need to be navigated? What sacrifices need to be made? And why is it worth the effort it takes to make it work? Let's turn now to these concerns.

YOUTH PARTICIPATORY ACTION RESEARCH IN THE CLASSROOM: MY JOURNEY

When I graduated from UCLA, I took a job teaching 11th-grade English at a high school in one of the South Los Angeles communities in which I had been working with the council students. It had been 5 years since I last held a full-time teaching job; in the interim, I was exposed to theories that transformed my understanding of systemic educational inequity and transformative critical pedagogies. I had written a dissertation exploring the ways that fellow high school English teachers in this community integrated civic discussion and action into their literacy practice. And I had become immersed in the practice of YPAR and been forever changed by the opportunity to lead the council community. I had learned so much; my perspective on teaching had expanded exponentially. So, what was I going to do differently the second time around?

I considered the challenges that I would face as I attempted to bring YPAR to my classroom. Instead of the 30 students of the council, I would now have 150 students across my five English classes. Instead of the freedom I enjoyed in the council to develop curriculum geared solely toward the needs of my students, I now would have to consider the need to explicitly address standards and the pressure of a high-stakes standardized test that students needed to pass to graduate. And finally, instead of the ability to take students around the city and state to collect data, I now would have to remain largely inside the school building. The pragmatist in me reasoned that while I might not be able to re-create the unique learning environment of the council, I could still work within the constraints I faced to fashion something meaningful that would flip the way that research traditionally was conceptualized in the English classroom.

As a faithful proponent of the backwards design approach to planning, I began by developing the provocative questions that I wanted my students to weigh and debate with me throughout the year and long after they had left my class. I settled on two essential questions for ELA 11:

1. How does literature both mirror our own experiences and provide windows onto the experiences of others?
2. How can we use our literacy skills to fight for justice in an often-unjust world?

Although at that point I had not yet arrived at the focus on critical civic empathy that guides this book, in hindsight I see that these questions speak to the two axes of humanization and social action. The first question referenced the power of imaginative texts to help us better understand ourselves and others (as explored in Chapter 1), while the second question served as a reminder of the role of literacy in civic engagement. Having these questions in place offered a rationale for the integration of YPAR into my classroom, which helped me explain and justify my pedagogical choices to my administrators.

My next step involved determining the scope of the YPAR project I wanted to create. I decided that instead of attempting to shoehorn YPAR into a 6 to 8 week unit, it would make more sense for me to design a year-long capstone project that would proceed alongside the more discrete sequence of instructional units. Though YPAR is flexible enough to adapt to a variety of contexts and constraints, my previous experience with the council, and my keen awareness of the length of time each step of the research process would take to complete as a result of the multiple demands of the school year, made a long-term plan feel right for me. I determined that the fall semester would be devoted entirely to writing research proposals, while the spring semester would focus on data collection, analysis, and the creation of findings presentations.

Because I was committed to ensuring that the project would feel integrated into the rest of the course rather than like an add-on, my next consideration was the design of my units and choice of focus texts that would connect to and foster the competencies needed for YPAR, including the ability to question assumptions, think critically, and take alternative perspectives. Since YPAR is grounded in taking a stance of inquiry toward society, I wanted to design an 11th-grade American literature course that took a stance of inquiry toward this country. Instead of moving chronologically through American literature, I organized thematic units based on enduring tensions in American life—the frictions that exist between the ideals and values of our nation. For instance, I began the year by considering a key democratic challenge—weighing the rights of the minority against the majority. I continued by exploring other binaries (e.g., freedom versus security, citizenship versus capitalism) and connecting each pair with focus texts that illustrated those themes (see Figure 3.5).

While I won't detail here the thinking behind my choice of each text on this list (or include the many supplemental texts that accompanied each of them), I do want to single out *Our America* as a mentor text especially well suited for introducing students to YPAR and getting reluctant readers engaged at the beginning of the school year. You'll remember this text as the one that Jerica Coffey read with her students (described in Chapter 1) to get them thinking about social reproduction and individual agency. I was so excited by the fact that this text was authored by teens and essentially shared their process of conducting research about their community that I decided to make it the very first text that students read in my course. My students were immediately drawn to the book's content and style; though its themes were complex, its language was inviting enough to help me identify and hook the students who were reading below grade level.

I helped my students understand YPAR by making reference to the steps that LeAlan and Lloyd, the authors of *Our America*, made in their book. As we read their vivid descriptions of their community and the challenges it faced, I introduced the concept of the problem statement, the part of a research report in which the context is laid to set up the research question. As we read about the statistics and data they included in their story to offer the reader a broader sense of context, I introduced the concept of the literature review and the need to situate a research project in the scholarship that has come before. And finally, as we read the quotes from the interviews that they conducted, I introduced the concept of methodology and helped students consider the various ways that information can be collected to address a research question.

Appendix C includes the research proposal template that I used with students and Appendix D offers a brief overview of various forms of data collection that I shared with students in class (which I accompanied with examples of each method in action).

Figure 3.5. My Focus Text Sets

Tensions in American Life	Focus Texts
Majority versus Minority	*Our America* by LeAlan Jones and Lloyd Newman with David Isay
	Fences by August Wilson
Freedom versus Security	*The Crucible* by Arthur Miller
	Zoot Suit by Luis Valdez
Citizenship versus Capitalism	*The Great Gatsby* by F. Scott Fitzgerald
	Nickel and Dimed by Barbara Ehrenreich

At this point, students were prepared to begin thinking about the topics they wanted to research in their own American lives. Though we began with individual brainstorming, I knew that I wanted to eventually move students into groups of inquiry, both to honor the collaborative nature of YPAR and to stave off the impossible task of managing 150 research projects. Although I initially worried that students' research interests would be so diverse as to make groupings difficult, I found that each class generated similar lists of concerns, which facilitated the creation of interest-driven teams. The most common community challenges that my students wanted to explore included neighborhood violence/gangs, teen pregnancy, drugs/ alcohol, and educational opportunity.

Each Friday during the fall semester, I would offer seminars to move students forward in designing their projects; topics included conceptualizing research questions, understanding social theories, searching for community data, and choosing appropriate data collection methods. After school, I reached out to local nonprofit organizations that worked on students' research topics in the community and arranged for individuals to come to our class as guest speakers and offer themselves as interview subjects.

By the time the spring semester rolled around, students had solidified their proposals and were ready to move into data collection. While I could not take students out of the building during the school day to collect data, I set deadlines for when students needed to bring in data that they gathered during after-school hours; we found that interviews with family members and friends worked well, as did observational photography that students could do with their smart phones. Because most of the groups were interested in gathering their classmates' opinions on their topics, we developed a survey that we distributed to the entire student body during our school's advisory period—each group collaborated on a set of items related to its particular topic. Once we had collected hundreds of responses, I developed seminars to help students understand the data and disaggregate them by gender, grade level, race, and other relevant factors. See Appendix E for our survey questions.

Although my description might make this process sound idyllic, it was marked by a series of challenges. Students transferred in and out of class during the school year, disrupting group cohesion. Facilitating groupwork, which is challenging under any conditions, became even more difficult when responsibilities for gathering data outside of class were involved. The entire project was put on hold for 2 months in the spring when all teachers were required to concentrate solely on the upcoming state tests. Invariably, YPAR projects speed up as external deadlines approach, which usually means that data analysis is rushed as students strive to organize final presentations. Although I originally had envisioned a large community showcase event to celebrate students' findings, the hectic nature of the end of the school year forced me to drastically scale back to classroom presentations.

Nevertheless, many of my students shared with me during self-assessments that engaging in YPAR was one of the most meaningful experiences of their junior year. They were impressed by the respect that their family members and school administrators showed them when they requested interviews, and, like the council students, they felt empowered by the idea that they had valuable knowledge to contribute to public dialogues about community challenges. Derek, a student who had struggled throughout the year with other class assignments but had blossomed through engaging in YPAR, wrote, "I never thought that I could be an expert on anything or that research could be about real life."

GETTING STARTED WITH YOUTH PARTICIPATORY ACTION RESEARCH IN VARIOUS CONTEXTS

Because the theory and practice of YPAR are so foundationally grounded in challenging hegemonic views of knowledge and amplifying nondominant voices, this very reasonable question arises: Is YPAR something in which only minoritized students should engage? The answer is: No. YPAR represents an approach to knowledge production that privileges the perspectives of youth writ large as a category of people whose expertise often is minimized. At the same time, however, as with any consciousness-raising practice, special considerations must be taken into account when engaging in this activity with different groups of students.

As I've explored throughout this chapter, what separates YPAR from traditional research is the interrogation of dominant perspectives and the embracing of alternative and indigenous forms of knowledge. This means that if you are engaging in YPAR with young people whose perspectives are dominant in society or whose ways of knowing are already celebrated, some attention must be dedicated to teaching about critical social theory in order to help students understand the nature of power and privilege in society and their relationship to these concepts. Such dialogue is crucial to avoid reducing the process to a simple one of asking a question, gathering data, and sharing results, which in effect would rob it of its transformative potential.

By the same token, if you are engaging in YPAR with young people from minoritized communities, just as much teaching must be done—but from a different starting point. I have found that young people who have grown up listening to dominant narratives about their communities—narratives that often highlight problems and risks—often begin to internalize deficit-oriented views of themselves and their peers and in turn castigate rather than celebrate where they come from. The YPAR process needs to make transparent how these negative portrayals become the norm, by introducing concepts like social reproduction and hegemony and then helping students recognize their ability to move beyond what novelist Chimamanda Ngozi Adichie (2009) calls "the danger of a single story" through counter-storytelling grounded in community cultural wealth.

YPAR should always involve a bit of productive discomfort because it challenges the very norms that govern what we believe to be true and how we come to know—processes that are integral to our identities. YPAR is meant to shake us up and broaden our horizons, and that involves some growing pains.

The profoundly contextual nature of YPAR makes it difficult to condense into easy how-to guides with clear steps to follow. Civic education initiatives that bear some resemblance to YPAR, and that attempt to provide such guides, have begun popping up around the country. I urge you to be wary of such programs because they often sidestep the difficult conversations about knowledge, positionality, and power that distinguish YPAR from other forms of social action. In order to foster critical civic empathy, the process needs to go hand in hand with considerations of epistemology—the nature and purpose of knowledge.

At the same time, you should not feel paralyzed by the intensity of the YPAR process to the point where you turn away from it. Instead, I suggest starting small—instead of organizing an entire unit of YPAR inquiry, perhaps organize some lessons asking students to probe their assumptions about how they know something to be true. Critical media literacy is a great starting point for gaining the competencies appropriate to YPAR, because of the ways that media products skillfully utilize tropes and logic to create schemas of the world for consumers to buy into (both literally and figuratively). In the case of the Crockett High School students, critiques of a documentary film provided the spark that ignited their YPAR project. You could use a similar strategy as a starting point by asking your students: How is your community portrayed in the news or in popular culture? Whether your students are focused on local community issues or broader investigations of gender stereotypes or consumer culture, analysis of local, national, and international media sources is a great way to generate interest and kick off a larger inquiry.

Reading up on YPAR, seeking out folks in your local context who may already be familiar with it, and finding ways to engage in inquiry yourself are low-stakes ways to begin the journey. From this point, you could try tweaking the summative assessment for a unit you already teach to give students opportunities to demonstrate their knowledge in authentic ways or in alternative formats. Instead of (or in addition to) a persuasive essay, perhaps invite community members to participate in a town hall meeting on your focus topic. Or organize a curated collection of student photos. Once you give yourself permission to think beyond the grammar of schooling, you might be surprised at what is possible.

CONCLUSION

Though the idea that reading and responding to literature can foster empathy has a great deal of precedent in scholarship and popular culture, the idea that conducting research can accomplish that same goal is more of a conceptual leap. I believe this cognitive dissonance occurs because of the imaginative, intuitive, and relational nature of empathy and the way that we associate these qualities with creativity but not with science. We understand storytelling as an act of imagination and connection, but do not consider research to qualify as storytelling the same way that novels do. YPAR is a practice that pushes us forward in our understanding and enactment of critical civic empathy because it reminds us that what we tend to consider factual or objective is just another instantiation of storytelling and that the process of knowledge production can help (or hinder) the cause of humanizing communities and providing the basis for transformative social action.

When educators tell me their hesitations about experimenting with YPAR in their practice, one of their most frequent concerns is how students will respond to the enormity and the seemingly intractable nature of many of the social problems they study. They ask, Won't doing YPAR make students angry or depressed or discouraged? And I always respond the same way—first, students already know a great deal about these issues viscerally, so furthering this understanding by introducing more data or disciplinary vocabulary about them will hardly be shocking. I often tell my students that they already know what complex social theories like social reproduction mean—I'm just giving them some new terms to use to describe that knowledge. Far from discouraging them, showing students the respect to delve into these issues with them and offering them the trust to conduct and share their own inquiries can provide students with a motivating sense of agency. YPAR gives students access to more nuanced structural social perspectives and an avenue for doing something about the problems in their communities, instead of blaming themselves or their community members for those problems.

As a result, YPAR creates critical civic empathy on multiple levels—students can better empathize with themselves and their communities, and adults can better empathize with their students and with members of communities to which they do not directly belong. The collaborative and action-oriented knowledge that emerges from both the process and findings of YPAR guides us toward understanding the ways in which power and positionality characterize all aspects of the research endeavor and the emptiness of research that does not seek to improve the lives of all it touches. YPAR is a profoundly democratic practice that operates on the hopeful premise that truth emerges when all members of a society can express their expertise, and that this truth can help society overcome even its most entrenched challenges. That is the kind of hope that should animate our classrooms.

DISCUSSION/REFLECTION QUESTIONS

1. What have your experiences with the research process been like as a student and/or as an educator? What rules did you follow? Which sources were considered wells of expertise?

2. What opportunities do you offer your students to be experts in your classroom? How might you introduce or expand these opportunities?

3. Where might you find openings in your courses to integrate YPAR projects?

CHAPTER 4

Navigating the Digital Public Sphere Through Connected Learning (and Teaching)

If you have ever read the comments that follow many online news stories and blog posts or witnessed a disagreement on social media boil over into a full-blown war of words, you likely have felt at least a flicker of despair about the state of public discourse (and perhaps humanity itself). How can people be so cruel? Would they be as brazen with their insults if the people they were criticizing were standing right in front of them? The ubiquity of trolling, bullying, and just plain meanness on digital media sites has elicited a question that CNN used as the headline for a 2011 article: Is the Internet killing empathy?

Indeed, even as public discourse about the Internet remains focused mostly on the power and potential of its capabilities, concern has begun to emerge about its consequences for users' lives, specifically in terms of relational trust and perspective-taking. Though the scientific research is uneven, a number of studies have suggested that online activities (e.g., gaming, posting on social media sites) can damage our social interactions in both virtual and in-person spaces by reducing our ability to pick up on nonverbal cues like facial expressions and body language in others (Konrath, O'Brien, & Hsing, 2011; Turkle, 2012). Research also has suggested that the seeming anonymity of online interaction can desensitize us to others' distress and that the curated showcases of others' lives can negatively affect our own self-esteem, even as we trend toward increased levels of narcissism (Heirman & Walrave, 2008).

These findings have led to calls for restricted amounts of "screen time" and intense surveillance and scrutiny of young people's online activities, at the same time that messages continue to proliferate about how their mastery of digital tools is the key to economic success in a globalized society. This tension creates a tricky situation in schools as educators seek both to protect young people from potential danger and prepare them for life beyond the classroom walls (Kellner & Share, 2007). Many seek to triage the situation by labeling some forms of engagement as off limits while encouraging others. Facebook = banned, but coding = necessary! Snapchat = distraction, but

Google Classroom = learning tool! (American Association of School Librarians, 2012). Also increasing in popularity in schools are "digital citizenship" curricula (Ribble, 2015) that seek to train young people about how to act in online spaces in order to minimize risk and maximize privacy. Consider how many times you've seen teachers make requests online for others to share posts to teach students how easily their words can "go viral."

Although I certainly do not seek to minimize the very real challenges raised by digitally mediated social interactions, particularly with regard to children, I do suggest that much of the panic about the decline of empathy in the digital age has roots not necessarily in the digital tools themselves, but in the push toward isolated individualism over the past several decades in all areas of public life, including democratic engagement. As with other revolutionary communication advances (e.g., the printing press, television), the Internet is a tool for us to make of it what we will. While we must acknowledge and wrestle with its potential to magnify our worst impulses and replicate our entrenched norms of behavior, we should not do so at the expense of exploring its potential to cultivate the best in us and introduce new forms of interaction and learning.

And what is it that the Internet has allowed us to do on a never-before-imagined scale? Connect across time and space. Of course, with the possibility of connection inevitably comes opposite forces of conflict and disengagement, but I argue that focusing on the concept of connection and exploring the ways that the affordances of digital technology allow us to engage with one another in novel ways can help disrupt our traditional ideas of what school needs to look like and foster empathy for the experiences of those both near and far in pursuit of the common goals of equity and justice.

In this chapter, I explore an educational framework that seeks to capitalize on the unique potential of digital media tools to foster connection between young people and among the various home, peer, school, and community contexts of their lives. The approach is appropriately called connected learning. Although I will delve into the specifics of connected learning throughout the chapter, I first give a brief definition as offered by Dr. Mimi Ito (2013) and her collaborators in their introductory report on the concept:

> [Connected learning] advocates for broadened access to learning that is socially embedded, interest-driven, and oriented toward educational, economic, or political opportunity. Connected learning is realized when a young person is able to pursue a personal interest or passion with the support of friends and caring adults, and is in turn able to link this learning and interest to academic achievement, career success, or civic engagement. (p. 4)

You may notice that technology was not mentioned at all in this definition, which was intentional on the part of the authors; while the report goes on to explain the unique affordances of digital media in supporting the aims of connected learning, the model is focused primarily on the quality of learning rather than on the tools that foster it. I suggest that this focus is crucial for us educators as technology becomes more and more prevalent across the educational (and every other social) landscape—we have to think first about the kinds of experiences that we want students to have and then find the tools needed to make those experiences happen, rather than starting from the premise that we must always somehow use technology in every lesson. Connected learning indeed can take place without any technology use at all—although, if it is used thoughtfully and creatively, technology often can deepen the scope and impact of that learning exponentially.

In this chapter, I share why I believe connected learning offers educators a more productive way to think about technology integration than the popular 21st-century learning model. I then suggest the need to articulate a model of connected teaching and name the competencies and commitments needed to make connected learning opportunities available to all students—competencies that embody critical civic empathy in action. Finally, I analyze examples of connected teaching in action and offer suggestions for becoming a connected educator in your own context.

MY INTRODUCTION TO CONNECTED LEARNING

I was introduced to the connected learning framework at a professional development session sponsored by the National Writing Project (NWP), an organization that has taken a leadership role in translating the theory of connected learning into practice with classroom teachers. Though the entire report is available as a free ebook online at dmlhub.net/publications/connected-learning-agenda-for-research-and-design/, I find the graphic in Figure 4.1, which encapsulates the guiding principles of connected learning, to be the most compelling way to grasp the approach and explain it to others.

The darker circles represent orientations toward learning. When learning is *interest-powered* and relevant to students' lives, students are more energized and motivated to engage in higher-order thinking skills. When learning is *peer-supported*, it leverages the everyday energy and exchanges between friends and classmates to foster collaboration, sharing, and problem-solving in a virtuous feedback loop. And when learning is *academically oriented*, it engages with the knowledge, skills, and habits of mind valued in formal academic settings and helps students see connections between their interests and possible career pathways.

You may be saying to yourself, "Sure, this just makes sense." Indeed, when I first saw these learning principles I thought that they were simply foundations of good teaching. Nevertheless, I think it is important to articulate and constantly remind ourselves how important these principles are, particularly when the pressures of high-stakes testing and accountability

Figure 4.1. Connected Learning Principles

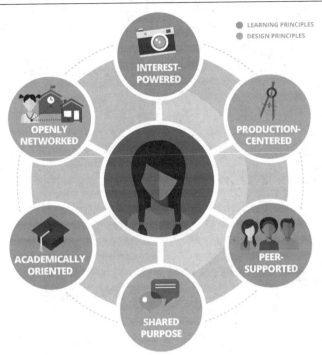

mandates cause us to begin drifting away from them—more on how to manage those soon.

Importantly, the learning principles are paired with a set of design principles that encourage us to consider the nature of the educational opportunities we construct for our students. When learning is *production-centered*, it encourages students to move from passively consuming information to actively creating artifacts of their knowledge, which requires those higher-order thinking skills. When learning is *openly networked*, it moves beyond the walls of the classroom space and into the wider world, where it gains authenticity and relevance and becomes accessible to a wide audience that can take it up and apply it in novel ways. And when learning has a *shared purpose*, it encourages participants to consider the "why" of their work as well as the "what" and offers a key reminder that learning does not occur in a vacuum but within a diverse and complex civic context.

I find that the design principles are what really give innovative shape and direction to the learning principles; they are also the entry point for thinking about the affordances of technology in purposeful ways. New media platforms offer a wide range of expressive possibilities that by their very nature involve production and interactivity, whether through Twitter chats or YouTube videos. They allow young people to find support and outlets for their interests far beyond their physical locations and to manifest their learning in a variety of forms and styles. And, while there is much to be concerned about when it comes to corporate-controlled online media, digital spaces can encourage and promote a wider multiplicity of voices in the public sphere than do more traditional forms of media like newspapers and TV shows. So, again, though technology is not the core of connected learning, it is a tool with the power to foster connection at a scale that cannot help but transform how we think about learning and the opportunities we offer our students.

The original connected learning report included a series of short case studies that highlighted various examples of the approach in action. The majority of these case studies discussed activities that young people engaged in outside of formal school spaces, including fan fiction writing, Minecraft, and so on, and noted the uneven response that their interests elicited in class; though some teachers found ways to connect these activities to coursework, most did not. Except for the example of one innovative secondary school, formal schooling was characterized as largely reluctant to embrace connected learning. As I mentioned in Chapter 3, the grammar of schooling is persistent and resistant to change. Connected learning, with its focus on making, collaboration, and open access, does not mesh well with the strict categorization by grade level and subject matter that characterizes much formal public education—to say nothing of the one-size-fits-all nature of most assessments.

As a result of these differences, connected learning first gained most traction in out-of-school learning communities such as libraries, museums, and nonprofit programs. My colleague Antero Garcia (2014) became concerned that if public schools were left out of the conversations around connected learning, it would reinforce the narrow practices taking place within them and create a divide in which innovation could happen only outside their doors. He knew that despite the constraints facing teachers in formal learning spaces, many were developing innovative learning opportunities for their students and bringing connected learning to life in their own contexts; indeed, many of the teachers affiliated with NWP were included in this number. With support from NWP and the Digital Media and Learning Research Hub at the University of California, Irvine (which recently has developed into a new Connected Learning Lab), Antero brought together a group of colleagues—including me—to share how various NWP educators were bringing connected learning to life in classroom spaces. *Teaching in the Connected Learning Classroom* (available as a free ebook online at dmlhub. net/publications/teaching-connected learning-classroom/) provides links to educators' stories in their own words, along with resources and analysis about how connected learning gives a language to what they were already doing with their students.

Though the principles of connected learning overlap and classroom projects invariably touch upon multiple principles at once, each chapter of the ebook concentrates on one principle at a time and how teachers embodied its commitments. Delving into each of the projects is beyond the scope of this chapter, but Figure 4.2 indicates the range of activities that teachers developed with their students.

The common thread across all of these projects was the creativity exhibited by the teachers to acknowledge but also push through the constraints that they faced in their formal settings in order to develop powerful connected learning experiences for their students. I think of this creativity as a form of pragmatic agency—instead of reducing expectations in the face of constraints, these teachers persevered with the resources at their disposal while maintaining the sense of purpose and possibility that challenges the traditional grammar of schooling.

Since the publication of the ebook, I have conducted many professional development sessions to introduce teachers to the ideas of connected learning. I usually start by displaying a quote that often is attributed to author Herman Melville—"A thousand fibers connect us to our fellow men"—and then asking teachers to write about what they feel it means to be connected and to whom or what they feel connected. During a workshop with the UCLA Writing Project, some teachers responded:

"To be connected means sharing a common experience, a thought, or feeling. I am connected to physical things like members of my family, friends, and colleagues but I am also connected to intangible things like feelings and emotions that could either be felt by me or shared with another person. Not like Facebook connected but really connected."

"Being connected means to be interrelated and independent. You are connected to family because they help you and vice versa. You are related to each person differently but yet still a family. It means that nothing is isolated or alone. Nothing exists or came into being on its own."

We used these statements as a way in to the language of connected learning and a jumping off point for considering small moves teachers could make to get started with integrating one or two of the principles into their practice. Although teachers are largely excited about the model, they often share with me some of the barriers they anticipate facing in response to it when they return to their school sites. The most common concerns that I hear are (1) school leaders want to see students using devices each time they walk into a classroom, but only on activities that conform to traditional school practices such as word processing; and (2) school leaders are wary of any digital activity that might put students into contact with the public in ways that are not highly controlled.

These concerns highlight the pitfalls of locating promise (or blame) in technology tools rather than focusing on the purposes for which they are

Figure 4.2. Examples of Connected Learning Classroom Activities

Connected Learning Principle	Classroom Activities
Interest-driven learning	Blogging, feature filmmaking, zine-making
Peer-supported learning	iMovie-making, documentary filmmaking, multimedia composing
Academically oriented learning	Gaming, Google Apps, comics/graphic novel–making
Production-centered learning	Narrative gaming, programming, critical media production
Openly networked learning	VoiceThread letter-writing, digital storytelling, museum-based learning
Shared-purpose learning	Digital storytelling, service learning, hip-hop literacies

being put to use—the conversation becomes about the tools rather than the pedagogy. This takes us back to the beginning of this chapter and the idea that technology is responsible for a decline of empathy in our society; holding tools responsible for what humans do with them glosses over and distracts attention from the ways that American society writ large is embracing more individualistic and atomistic views of education, democracy, and social interactions in general. Instead of considering how our *uses* of technology might be causing negative effects, we seek to regulate the tools themselves, which can lead to proposed solutions such as bans of particular sites or the use of firewalls to keep students away from social media altogether. For instance, instead of tackling the deeper issue of why many individuals feel the need to curate idealized personas and shame others on platforms like Facebook or Instagram, it seems easier to simply ban students from accessing Facebook or Instagram at school. This relates to the aforementioned risk-focused nature of many digital citizenship curricula; though they may sidestep challenges in the short term, they do not help students learn to navigate the possibilities (and challenges) of the online environment that promises to continue shaping all of our lives in fundamental ways.

Teaching students that they can engage individually with others on the Internet in positive or negative ways promotes the individual view of empathy without the broader context about the ways that power and privilege play out through digital communication and without a frame of reference for collective democratic action. I believe that connected learning can set the stage for considerations of critical civic empathy. In order to tease out the possible relationships between digital media and empathy, I want to offer a brief comparison of connected learning and a much more common approach to technology integration called 21st-century learning. This comparison demonstrates the orientations and practices necessary to practice critical civic empathy in digital learning contexts.

CULTIVATING CONNECTIONS BEYOND THE 21ST-CENTURY MODEL

While you may not have heard the term *connected learning* before, I am sure that you've heard of *21st-century learning*—the term is nearly inescapable. In fact, the modifier *21st-century* is applied freely to any number of people and objects in education, including 21st-century students, 21st-century schools, 21st-century literacies, and a 21st-century society. The prevalence of the term can be traced to the Partnership for 21st Century Learning, a network of business, government, and education organizations that advocate for schools to focus on skills that they deem necessary for success in a globalized economy. The skills that they promote have become known as the four Cs and include creativity, communication, collaboration, and critical thinking (Partnership for 21st Century Learning, 2016).

On the surface, this model seems rather compatible with the connected learning approach; after all, it is easy to draw parallels between principles of interest-driven or openly networked learning and the skills of creativity and collaboration. I suggest, however, that the two approaches differ sharply in their views of technology and of pedagogical purpose; whereas 21st-century learning is oriented toward individual economic advancement and the promise inherent in technological devices, connected learning is committed to collective civic advancement and the ways that technology can support innovative and equitable forms of learning.

The vision statement on the website of the Partnership for 21st Century Learning states that "tomorrow's leaders, workers, and citizens" need 21st-century skills to support "innovation in our economy and the health of our democracy." In examining this rhetoric, it becomes clear that it is attempting to create parallels between economic success and the maintenance of democratic life, as if a causal relationship exists between individuals being financially successful and democracy being robust. This conflation of economics with democracy is the hallmark of neoliberal thought, which characterizes public life in financial terms—citizens are consumers, public life is the free market, and individuals are repositories of human capital (Brown, 2015; Harvey, 2007).

I contend that this neoliberal thinking is driving many of the practices being put in place around technology in our schools. According to the 21st-century learning model, technology is the engine that fuels the global economy; it breaks down borders and allows for a flow of information that drives trade and cultural exchange. The model argues that students must master technological tools in order to be competitive in this globalized context; as a result, the technological tools are glorified more than the pedagogy associated with them (Griffin, McGaw, & Care, 2011). This logic that students need to be using technology tools as much as possible drives the quest in many districts to get devices into the hands of every student and, as the teachers in my UCLA Writing Project workshop noted, push for those devices to be used all the time, regardless of whether a particular learning goal can be best served by them.

Unlike the 21st-century learning model, in which education and technology are interpreted through a narrowly economic lens and in isolation from the complex sociopolitical context in which they reside, the connected learning model offers a vision of learning and literacy that reclaims a public purpose to schooling and encourages dialogue and collaboration across sectors for the benefit of students and communities (Jenkins, 2013). Rather than locating power in technology tools, it highlights the ecology of learning created by those tools (Baker-Doyle, 2017). This distinction is best exemplified in the way that each model defines literacy. Twenty-first-century learning argues that students need opportunities to engage in "new literacies" made possible by technology; that is, the mechanics of reading, writing, listening, and speaking involving digital devices rather than pen and paper. Also dubbed "digital literacies," these skills often involve the use of social media, content creation platforms, and presentation tools.

Connected learning, on the other hand, draws upon the field of new literacy studies, an approach that stresses literacy as a social practice rather than a set of technical skills (Coiro, Knobel, Lankshear, & Lue, 2012; Lankshear & Knobel, 2003). Rather than focusing on the affordances of particular new literacy tools, new literacy studies use a multiliteracies framework to examine the expanded range of expressive forms made possible by these tools and the ways that they can be leveraged to foster equity and open up new "social futures" for all young people (New London Group, 1996).

These two models represent vastly divergent orientations toward literacy that have major implications for literacy classroom instruction and for the development of empathy. Because connected learning requires critical thought about the work that it takes to actually forge connections between and among young people and with potential co-learners of all ages, it is concerned with equity. Connected learning views equity not in terms of students' access to digital devices, but in terms of their access to authentic, relevant, and engaging learning experiences geared toward civic engagement rather than mere economic success. On our typology of empathy, these commitments push connected learning toward mutual humanization and social action. We soon will explore specific examples of this equity focus in action, but it essentially involves asking questions during instructional planning such as: Whose voices are present (and missing) in this activity? How can we introduce divergent perspectives? How is this subject relevant to society today? Questions about the appropriate tools for learning are secondary.

I want to reiterate the point made earlier that the amplifying power of technology cuts both ways—just as it can foster connection on a scale never before seen, so can it foster hate and divisiveness. It also can be (and is being) warped by neoliberal ideology to reinforce individualistic and capitalistic values. The rise of hate speech in online spaces, along with the prevalence of fake news and echo chambers (as discussed in Chapter 2), reminds us that we must remain vigilant about how we leverage the affordances of these tools—and acknowledge their limitations—if we want to use them to pursue the development of critical civic empathy.

So, how can we go about integrating connected learning into our practice? I believe that it requires us to do some rethinking about the nature of teaching.

FROM CONNECTED LEARNING TO CONNECTED TEACHING: A NECESSARY STEP FORWARD

I am lucky to know some amazing teachers. I know teachers who are throwing open the doors of their classrooms and partnering with community organizations, libraries, and museums to expand students' learning opportunities. I know teachers who are flipping the hierarchical teacher–student relationship on its head to allow students to take the lead in their learning. I know teachers who are linking their students to networks that discuss and take action on the most pressing issues of the day. These teachers embody connected learning in action.

NWP's Educator Innovator network (educatorinnovator.org/) has been documenting the work of educators using the connected learning approach across the country, from the LRNG Challenge (www.lrng.org/innovators) to the Connected Learning Alliance (clalliance.org/). These resources are a huge source of inspiration and a showcase of powerful learning in action.

But, having once been a new teacher myself, I began to realize that these resources also can be a bit intimidating. These teachers all seem so *amazing* —magical, even. They make incredible learning happen and their students seem constantly enthralled. Doubts can begin to creep in for us mere mortal teachers—could I ever do something like this? Surely these teachers are far more skilled and successful than I could ever be.

And then it hit me—understanding the *why* of connected learning is easy; understanding the *how* is much more complicated. Teachers need opportunities to see the process through which their colleagues decide to go out on that limb for the first time and experiment with new ways of thinking and doing. In order to increase the spread and impact of connected learning, it is urgent that we begin to articulate a model of *connected teaching*.

Pockets of teachers and teacher educators are beginning this generative work. One burgeoning example is the Connected Learning in Teacher Education group led by Kira Baker-Doyle at Arcadia University (learn more at sites.google.com/view/cl-in-te). I've also been talking to teachers and combing through existing resources to try to pinpoint some of the key moves that need to be made to embrace connected learning in practice. In almost all of my exploration, teachers who have experimented with connected learning have identified for me key moments in which they turned their back on what they previously had internalized about what it meant to be a teacher and took a chance on something new. I think that it is crucial to identify the ingrained assumptions of what a teacher does and who a teacher is so that we then can deconstruct them and build something new.

Here are some of the assumptions about teaching that I've uncovered in my conversations.

Teachers work (mostly) alone and (mostly) with one subject area.

Even though free-range learning often engages knowledge and skills from multiple disciplines at once, the majority of schools continue to use the early-20th-century model of separating learning into the discrete subject areas of English, history, math, and science. They also continue to place a single teacher in a classroom responsible for a single subject area, stifling possibilities for integrated, cross-subject projects.

Teachers possess the knowledge and skills that students need to be taught.

Paulo Freire called it the "banking model" of education—the idea that students are empty vessels waiting for all-knowing teachers to deposit knowledge into their brains. This model fails to consider young people as experts and maintains a power hierarchy in the classroom that prevents students' interests, passions, and capabilities from being taken seriously in academic learning.

Teachers control the learning experience—its design, implementation, and evaluation.

In my first years as a teacher, I learned quickly that administrators valued control above almost all else; regardless of what students were learning, as long as they were quiet, in their seats, and following directions, I was succeeding as an educator. Too often, we continue to resist the messiness that often accompanies learning in favor of strict order; we are taught to fear the chaos that might ensue if students are given the reins in the classroom.

Teachers need to maintain a divide between the classroom and the wider world.
As discussed earlier, many school leaders are eager to enforce strong divides between classrooms and public spaces in the interest of protecting students from risk. This comes in the form of physically demarcating schools from the communities in which they exist through elaborate barriers, limiting fieldtrips outside of the classroom, and erecting firewalls to block particular websites.

Teachers need to keep their identities out of the classroom.
As I will discuss further in Chapter 5, the increasing standardization of pedagogy and curriculum promotes the idea that teachers are transmitters of content who are indistinguishable from one another. Their identities and interests are expected to be bottled up in order to present a façade of objectivity and neutrality. They do not reveal all of themselves to their students, just their teacher personas.

All of us have likely acted upon these assumptions at one time or another—they are deeply baked into our psyches as educators. Teachers who have begun to challenge these assumptions engage in alternative practices that begin to help us articulate the commitments of connected teaching (see Figure 4.3). These commitments and practices include:

COLLABORATION: Connected teachers work collaboratively.
Connected teachers establish partnerships, whether with the history teacher in the classroom next door, a local library or museum, or virtual networks from across the country. They embrace project-based learning that deconstructs the boundaries between subject areas.

CURIOSITY: Connected teachers bring an inquiry mindset to classroom practice.
Connected teachers do not shut down ideas because they seem like they will be difficult to realize, and they do not allow themselves to become trapped in routines over the years. They ask, "Why not?" and "How?" and let their curiosity lead them toward innovations in their practice.

COURAGE: Connected teachers give up some of their control over the learning experience.
Connected teachers give choice and freedom to their students to achieve learning goals in self-directed ways. They beat back the nagging voice in their head telling them that time will be wasted as students figure out their own learning pathways and embrace the uneven but exciting progress of authentic learning.

Figure 4.3. Connected Teaching Commitments

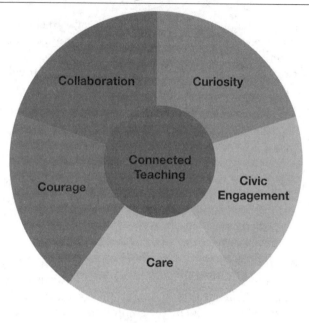

CIVIC ENGAGEMENT: Connected teachers engage their students in public life.

Connected teachers tear down their classroom walls by applying learning to real-life contexts, whether through researching a local policy, speaking to community elders, or communicating their views on controversial social issues. They create assessments that invite students to share their ideas with folks beyond the teacher.

CARE: Connected teachers share their interests and learning with their students.

Connected teachers model the habits of lifelong learners by sharing their passions with their students. They bring their entire selves to the classroom and make transparent the journeys that they undertake when learning something new to demonstrate the joys and frustrations of making something new.

Teachers need opportunities to cultivate these commitments in order to transition from conventional to connected forms of teaching. The process is certainly not easy or linear—we all will find ourselves wobbling at times—but being transparent about it, is the first step to radical transformation of practice.

I have put together a collection of 10 resources on The Current, NWP's repository of teaching ideas and lesson plans, in which teachers share in their own words the small moves and radical acts they have attempted in order to make their practice more connected. Though I encourage you to read them in their entirety (they can be found at thecurrent.educatorinnovator. org/collection/what-does-it-take-teach-connected learning), here is a taste of what teachers have made possible in their local contexts.

Collaboration. Teachers from four cities near former Japanese American internment sites came together in partnership with the National Park Service and the National Japanese American Historical Society to develop web-based K–12 curricula highlighting local place-based learning and the use of primary source documents. A Detroit public high school teacher partnered with a local media arts organization to help young people create multimodal texts about community issues that were meaningful to them.

Curiosity. A teacher participated in a massive open online course (MOOC) about connected learning and then sought to use technology in his own classroom to transform his teaching. A teacher educator structured an entire course around inquiry about the nature of literacy, reading, and power in a changing social and political context.

Courage. A high school English teacher experimented with Twitter in her classroom as a tool to facilitate Socratic seminars and explored the ways that risk-taking spurred innovations in her practice. An elementary school teacher organized online book clubs with his students using the Edmodo digital platform, being honest about the roadblocks and successes he encountered.

Civic Engagement. A teacher supported two students as they designed and tested a video game about a controversial issue that mattered to them— the perils of the cocoa industry. A group of teachers facilitated classroom discussions about controversial social issues involving race, violence, and the criminal justice system, and described handling the pain that these discussions can generate.

Care. Two high school teachers established a culture of care among their students by entrusting them with the responsibility to plan and implement a "bioethics" day that promoted humanization and empathy in science. A group of Black male educators reflected on the sense of love that brought them into the teaching profession and keeps them there at a time when there is such a shortage of teachers of color, highlighting the power of educator networks as sources of support and shared purpose.

There is no one way to approach connected learning, and these resources offer inspiration about the moves you can make with the resources you have available to you in your context.

ACTIVITIES TO JUMPSTART YOUR JOURNEY

Perhaps you feel that you need to engage in some inquiry of your own before you are ready to jump into the connected learning and teaching waters. Research shows that you are not alone, particularly when it comes to thinking about strategies for integrating technology into instructional practice in meaningful ways; as much as teachers may want to work with new tools, a large number of them do not have the time or support they need to research what is available and make the links to their existing curricula (Gray, Thomas, Lewis, & Tice, 2010; Purcell, Heaps, Buchanan, & Friedrich, 2013). All of us need to tinker with new ideas and tools in order to draw out their pedagogical potential.

I thought about these needs as I developed a New and Multimodal Literacies course for preservice teachers. I knew that I wanted to structure the course around the principles of connected learning and sought to develop activities that would give my students the time they needed to, as Mimi Ito put it in the title to one of her books, "hang out, mess around, and geek out" with digital media. You can engage in similar activities with your own professional networks in order to broaden your horizons about connected learning.

As a start, it is important to debunk once and for all the idea originally promoted by Marc Prensky back in 2001 that young people today are "digital natives" while the rest of us are "digital immigrants." Many before me have detailed the problems with this narrative (Bennett & Maton, 2010; Brown & Czerniewicz, 2010); suffice it to say that while young people may seem to have more facility with the newest digital apps and tools, they do not naturally or automatically know how to leverage these tools to achieve the kinds of academically oriented, peer-supported, and interest-driven learning outcomes that the tools can facilitate. That takes dedicated pedagogy and a mindset change among educators about what the young people in their lives actually do and think about in terms of technology.

I attempted to encourage this mindset change in my preservice teachers by asking them to partner with a young person and actually talk to that person about his or her experiences with technology. They interviewed young people about the similarities and differences in how they used technology in and out of school and encouraged the young people to share examples of their online literacy practices in multiple spaces—everything from Facebook posts and Snaps to Google Docs and Kahoot quizzes.

The results of this inquiry were illuminating. One of my students was dismayed when her interviewee told her that teachers often posted worksheets and other activities on online platforms, which resulted in fewer class discussions and interactions as students simply completed the work that was posted. As the student wrote in response, "Teachers should not be sitting behind their desks allowing technology to take over for them completely. Students need to feel worthy of being interacted with." Another student's interviewee told her that when a teacher had students create Facebook profiles for characters in a novel, she and her friends found it "gimmicky." This instance caused the student to reflect on "the distinction between teachers using technology in meaningful ways and depending on it to carry weak lesson plans."

This experience forced my students to think twice about surface-level nods to technology and give more in-depth consideration to what it would mean to truly use the affordances of digital tools to transform learning in more authentic, relevant, and equitable ways. As usual, the wisdom of young people led the way. It was at this point that I introduced the idea of the Genius Hour project. This concept has been gaining traction across the educational landscape since teachers learned that some employees at tech companies like Google were permitted to spend a portion of their work time engaging in passion projects not directly related to their primary responsibilities. The rationale behind this practice was that when folks have the time and support to exercise their creativity and pursue their interests, they think in more creative ways—creativity that benefits the company through original thinking, motivation, and increased productivity. A quick online search reveals the multiple ways that educators are attempting to integrate Genius Hour into their schools, from spending 1 day a week on student-directed projects to dedicating weeks to extended investigations.

In my version of Genius Hour, I encouraged my students to choose new media tools that they wanted to explore in more depth. I insisted that the tools they choose not be designed intentionally for use in the classroom because too often educational technology is designed to conform to or reinforce the traditional logic of schooling. Instead, I wanted them to choose tools that had no formal link to education and then do the work themselves to determine the kinds of learning outcomes that these tools could support in creative ways. I also required them to choose tools with which they were not familiar so that they could document their journey of determining how the tools worked and what it felt like to learn to use them.

One student, Madeline, decided to indulge her interests in gaming and fiction writing by exploring Storium, an online storytelling community in which narratives are constructed collaboratively by a group of "players" who create "cards" describing character attributes and actions. Stories are advanced as the player-writers design scenarios and obstacles to which their fellow storytellers respond. Madeline recorded a YouTube video that she shared with the class in which she demonstrated the pre-made story worlds participants could enter, as well as her process of recruiting players into a narrative she wanted to start writing that was inspired by Shakespeare's *Hamlet* and that she titled "This Be Madness."

After experiencing the process of collaborating with folks she had just met online to design a narrative arc, Madeline praised the "infinite possibilities" she saw for integrating Storium into English classrooms. She explained that the site is "essentially getting students excited about writing with a game aspect that usual assignments do not have." She imagined that teachers could develop writing assignments about class readings and allow students to pick characters and game moves.

Importantly, this inquiry also helped students identify new media tools that might not transfer as well to classroom learning. William explored HitRecord, an online community in which users create and post writing, music, videos, and/or art in an open format for other users to build upon or remix. During his presentation, he showed the class the profile that he created on the site, as well as some original music he wrote, and led us through the procedures used on the site to create, remix, communicate, and collaborate around media products. While he enjoyed the practice of remixing, William was careful to consider the implications that HitRecord had for student privacy, noting that because all uploaded content became property of the site, could not be deleted, and could be manipulated by anyone, it easily could stray from learning goals and compromise students' intentions.

This process of exploration and play can help us break out of the traditional teaching mindset and offer some inspiration for experimenting with the tenets of connected learning and teaching (see Appendix F for the assignment and rubric). Only when we give ourselves the time and space to experience alternative forms of learning can we begin to challenge the grammar of schooling and bend the constraints of public education toward a more connected vision.

CONCLUSION

The next time that you hear a news report or read an editorial claiming that technology is fraying the social fabric and contributing to the downfall of empathy, step back and ask yourself—to what extent is technology being essentialized? And then remember that the "connection" in connected learning refers not so much to a quality inherent in technology as to a quality of humanity. The power of algorithms and digitally mediated corporate content certainly can facilitate individualism and isolation in increasingly powerful ways, but we also have the ability to leverage these tools for purposes that help us find common purpose while still recognizing the socially constructed positions we occupy. Connected learning and teaching insist that we seek the potential for critical civic empathy in an enormously powerful digital communication infrastructure.

DISCUSSION/REFLECTION QUESTIONS

1. Consider the policies and practices around technology use that exist at your school site. What narrative about technology is being told? Explore the possible 21st-century or connected learning elements and reflect on how students internalize this narrative.

2. Which of the connected learning principles resonate most with you? Which feel more difficult to implement?

3. What is a new media tool that you would like to explore in order to tease out its potential pedagogical uses? How could you structure your own Genius Hour experimentation?

4. Think about potential partners you could enlist in your local context to help you move from traditional to connected teaching. What small moves could you make to cultivate this partnership?

CHAPTER 5

Practicing What We Preach

Teachers as Civic Agents

The previous chapters have explored how classroom literacy practices, from literary response and debate to research and digital storytelling, can be oriented toward the development of critical civic empathy so that students can tackle a civic context of divisiveness and polarization with humanity and democratic spirit. This orientation does not simply exist inherently within the literacy practices themselves; as discussed, an activity like debate can just as easily lean toward reinforcing narrowly academic views of literacy. The commitments of the teacher are what make all the difference.

This chapter differs from the others in this book in that it does not focus *directly* on literacy practices in school and community learning contexts; instead, it takes a step back and encourages us teachers, whether we are just beginning our careers or working as seasoned veterans, to consider the commitments and values that guide us as we decide which literacy practices to introduce to our students. It asks us to think about our purpose and the various elements—standards, policies, and beliefs—that influence (or complicate) that purpose. And it shares research findings that can aid in this reflection.

Now I know that it can seem indulgent to reflect on our purpose when we want to stay focused on student needs. When I work with preservice teachers who are planning and delivering lessons for the first time, I am acutely aware that they want concrete strategies they can put into use *immediately*. I suggest, however, that it is equally important to step back and consider the political messages that our choice of strategies is sending so that we can take control of the content and nature of the messages being transmitted to students and better meet their civic needs.

Wait, did you realize that you are sending political messages through your teaching? As mentioned in Chapter 1, that word—*political*—makes many of us uncomfortable because it challenges the norms of objectivity and neutrality to which we have been conditioned to conform as teachers. Most immediately, it evokes the specter of partisan political proselytizing in the classroom; during the 2016 U.S. presidential election cycle, stories circulated in the national news media about teachers investigated or fired for expressing support for (or disapproval of) particular candidates or positions. The preoccupation with teachers being ideological blank slates has a long and complex history in the United States that relates to the status of public school educators as agents of the state and to the unique power that they wield to influence young minds (Journell, 2016).

These concerns relate to what researcher Hilary Janks (2012) calls "Politics" (with an uppercase P), which is the realm of formal institutional government and battles between Democrats and Republicans. Understandably, schools that are publicly funded do not want to be seen as telling students whom to vote for. But this is not the only form of politics relevant to education—there is also "politics" with a lowercase p, which refers to the ways that ideology is enacted in our everyday lives. The purpose of this distinction is to remind us that even when we are not engaging in the world of institutional partisan politics, we are still being political in the sense that we are promoting beliefs, values, and actions that have import in public life. As discussed in the Introduction, nearly every choice that we make as teachers is political; the texts that we include (or exclude) in our curricula, the topics we introduce (or ignore) for discussion, our assessment and grading criteria—all send messages about what should be valued in education and in the society for which that education is meant to prepare us (Nieto, 2006). If we profess to be apolitical by simply following to the letter the mandated curriculum in our districts and being as blank as automatons, that is in itself a political choice that supports the high-stakes, neoliberal accountability culture.

Instead of becoming dismissive or defensive about the ways that little-p politics explicitly and implicitly structures our teaching, I suggest acknowledging that it offers a welcome opportunity for reflection that allows us to become more conscious and intentional about the messages we send through our practice. If we hope to move our instruction toward (political) goals of mutual humanization and equitable, justice-oriented social transformation, we must be intentional and rigorous in our work.

This chapter explores the steps that we teachers must take in our professional *and* personal lives to prepare ourselves to teach toward critical civic empathy with our students. I discuss the importance of zeroing in on your sense of purpose as a literacy educator so that you can make content standards work for you instead of the other way around. I analyze the various purposes of literacy instruction present in national and professional literacy standards and detail the results of a survey that I conducted with high school English teachers about how they conceptualize the goals of their discipline.

I also explore, by returning to the experiences of the focus teachers from Chapter 1, the struggles inherent in pursuing a critical and civic approach to literacy instruction in an educational context driven by standardization and accountability. Conversations with these teachers demonstrate the sense of pragmatism necessary to manage the tensions and contradictions of striving toward equity and justice in a system that often seems at odds with these goals.

Finally, I consider how our personal behaviors as citizens relate to the activities we engage in with our students. Though we may be conditioned by society and schools to separate our teacher personas from our personal identities, the truth is that who we are invariably influences what and how we teach. I explore the results of another survey I helped conduct, this time with a nationally representative sample of high school English teachers, about how individual civic behaviors influence teachers' classroom practices.

In his final book, Paulo Freire (2007) described teachers as cultural workers and defined teaching as "a political act, an act of love and vision" (p. xxii). The aim of this chapter is to foster dialogue about the teacher dispositions needed to pursue the development of critical civic empathy in the classroom and, building on Freire's work, to situate teachers as civic workers in troubled times.

NAVIGATING COMPETING PURPOSES
OF LITERACY EDUCATION

Amid the whirlwind of possibilities for how literacy and citizenship can be conceptualized in classrooms, one constant remains—classroom teachers act as crucial mediators who facilitate for their students experiences that embody multiple, contradictory, and unavoidably politicized visions of the literate citizen. While policymakers, researchers, and politicians often prod teachers to adopt particular stances toward literacy and citizenship, implementation of policies at the classroom level takes on different forms based on the normative and political dimensions of each school and classroom (Oakes, 1992).

Despite the acknowledged importance of teacher beliefs to classroom practice and the implementation of policy reforms, particularly in the highly contested realm of literacy (O'Brien, Stewart, & Moje, 1995), there is very little research available that explores how teachers are making sense of the variety of directions in which their disciplines are being pushed and how their understandings of their mission translate into particular classroom practices. Although teachers often enact practices in their classrooms that diverge from their stated beliefs (Raymond, 1997), it nevertheless remains important to explore how teachers conceptualize the purposes of their discipline and how these purposes may be reflected or contradicted in their classroom practice (Fang, 1996; Pajares, 1992). Furthermore, it is important to include the voices of teachers in conversations about the future of their subject areas and seek out their opinions and ideas as professionals and public intellectuals.

This desire to privilege teachers' ideas about the purposes of literacy and the characteristics of good citizenship led me to develop an online survey aimed at analyzing the beliefs and classroom practices of approximately 300 high school English teachers from across the country. Because of the constraints of the survey design, White teachers, female teachers, and teachers with more than 3 years of experience were over-represented in my sample.

Before eliciting responses from teachers about their goals for literacy education, I analyzed existing documents to determinethe goals that policymakers and professional organizations developed and expected teachers to implement. I focused on two documents: the ELA Common Core State Standards, which were released by the National Governors Association in 2010 and, to date, have been adopted by all but eight states; and the Standards for the English Language Arts, a collection of voluntary standards released in 1996 in a joint effort by the two largest professional organizations of English teachers in the nation—the National Council of Teachers of English (NCTE) and International Reading Association (IRA), which has since been renamed the International Literacy Association (ILA). I detail my analysis here because I encourage you to take a similar critical eye to the visions of literacy instruction embedded in the standards that you use in your context.

My close reading of these documents led me to identify five stated purposes for the study of literacy in secondary school: preparation for postsecondary education, preparation for career advancement, preparation for democratic life, literary appreciation, and general enjoyment of reading, writing, listening, and speaking. While teachers invariably engage with all five purposes in complex and overlapping ways, I was interested in teasing out which goals spoke most powerfully to my survey respondents; as a result, I required teachers to do a forced ranking of the purposes, with 1 indicating highest importance and 5 indicating lowest importance.

The 304 respondents to my survey mostly placed college preparation at the top of their lists of purposes (see Figure 5.1). Considering the strong emphases within national content standards on college and career preparation, it is perhaps not surprising that teachers considered it their primary mission to help students develop the skills needed for postsecondary education. College readiness consistently is paired with career readiness in the standards; however, teachers assigned much less importance to career preparation when given the opportunity to consider it separately. Given the push for college preparation and the link between educational attainment and career advancement, teachers may associate the skills needed in the workplace with college attendance itself.

Teachers also assigned strong importance to fostering enjoyment in students for the foundational activities of English classes—reading, writing, listening, and speaking. Respondents found this goal much more compelling than that of instilling appreciation in students for the canon of what traditionally is considered "great" literature.

This finding may reflect the shift in approaches to teaching literature in the classroom over the course of the 20th century from cultural transmission, in which students were expected to absorb the "greatness" of classic

Figure 5.1. Teachers' Rankings of the Purposes of Education (by percent)

1 = Most Important; 5 = Least Important

Purpose of English Education	1	2	3	4	5	Mean Ranking
Developing skills for postsecondary education	27	22	21	18	13	2.69
Fostering enjoyment for reading, writing, listening, and speaking	24	24	20	19	13	2.73
Developing skills to participate in political and civic life	22	23	19	20	15	2.83
Developing skills for career advancement	15	17	20	16	31	3.32
Instilling appreciation for great works of literature	13	13	19	27	28	3.43

literature, to a model of new critical close reading and reader-response, in which close textual analysis and the feelings and opinions of the readers themselves take precedence in literary study (Appleman, 2009). It also may reflect the broadening of the English curriculum from a narrow selection of canonical texts to a wider range of multicultural and alternative texts, which in turn deconstructs the very notion of great books (as discussed in Chapter 1).

The goal of helping students to develop the necessary skills to participate in political and civic life ranked solidly in the middle of the pack among survey respondents—seemingly on teachers' radar, but not the primary goal of high school English education. I hypothesize that this may be partially due to the fact that social studies classes consistently are given much more attention than English classes as sites for political and civic learning—civic standards often are paired with social studies standards, and the focus on explicit instruction in law and government as a best practice in civic education creates further connections with instruction in history. As a result, English teachers may not see political and civic education as subjects within their purview or receive as much professional support in making connections between English and civics. Nevertheless, preparation for civic life ranked high enough on the list of purposes to warrant further exploration of these connections.

Because I acknowledge that forced ranking does not accurately capture the complex ideas that high school English teachers possess about the purposes of their discipline, I also gave survey respondents the option to write open responses to the question, "In your own words, what do you think are the purposes of high school English classes?" Of the 304 respondents, 252 chose to respond.

The open responses, though somewhat reflective of the forced ranking responses, added layers of complexity to my analysis of the ways that English teachers think about their profession. I analyzed the responses to create thematic categories based on repetition of words, phrases, and ideas (see Figure 5.2). The great majority of respondents provided responses that contained multiple themes. By far the most common of these themes was a focus on helping students develop literacy skills—78% of open responses made specific mention of skills in general or of reading, writing, listening, or speaking skills more specifically. One teacher's response sums up this theme succinctly: "Increase the literacy of students. Teach strategies for close reading and comprehension of nonfiction texts/documents. Teach strategies for writing and grammar."

As discussed throughout the book, English is arguably one of the more skill-based disciplines that students encounter in high school—unlike the disciplines of history and science, in which content is specific, English teachers have the choice of a myriad of texts with which to reinforce literacy skills; indeed, standards give lists of suggested texts but provide English teachers with substantial discretion in terms of the content used to meet skill-based standards. In light of this situation, the focus on skills is quite expected, although it raises the question of what those skills are being put in service of.

As I analyzed the responses, I focused on the (small) number of teachers who engaged with civic and political goals for their classes. As one teacher wrote, "I want my students to become knowledgeable, to be capable of thinking critically about the world around them, and to communicate their thoughts, opinions, and feelings well in a democratic society. I believe I am to facilitate their success in becoming responsible and vital citizens in America." Another teacher echoed these themes: "High school English classes provide the means by which students can acquire the skills, understanding of human complexity through literary analysis, and communication acumen to become authentic citizens of the world." One teacher even quoted a Founding Father: "Like Jefferson, I agree that an educated citizenry is the most important tool we have to support our democracy."

In a category that I deemed qualitatively different from the development of good citizens, some respondents expressed the development of good people as a purpose for high school English education. Fourteen percent of open responses spoke of the way that English courses could promote "compassion," "self-esteem," "empathy," and "understanding of our shared

Figure 5.2. Thematic Categories for Teachers' Open Responses About the Purposes of High School English Education

Category	Percentage of Open Responses
Literacy Skills	78
Lifelong Learning	34
Love/Appreciation for Literature	34
Communication	26
Critical Thinking	21
Civic and Political Life	17
Good Personhood	14
College/Career Preparation	14
Digital Media/Technology	6
Critical Literacy	6

humanity." They articulated beliefs that English classes could "promote tolerance," "activate a love of beauty and virtue," and simply "help students become better people." I found it important to tease out separate themes for good personhood and good citizenship because of the more collective and politicized nature of the citizenship responses.

Critical conceptions of literacy were also in the minority among teachers' responses, but they represented a powerful strain of thought revealing how teachers are translating this theory into practice. Some teachers saw literacy in terms of student empowerment, speaking of "giving students a voice," "empowering students through various forms of communication," and "empowering our young people to believe in the power of their own personal and cultural stories." Some teachers focused on literacy as a guard against manipulation—one argued that students need literacy skills in order to recognize "truth, lies, and bias," and another wrote that students need "knowledge of the power of language so that they may protect and advocate for themselves." In an echo of Paulo Freire, several teachers spoke of enabling students to "critically read the world" and "effect change in the world." One teacher aptly summed up the relationship of literacy to political and social change:

All of these skills are for the purpose of communicating effectively in personal, professional, and civic life so that students are able to participate actively in political and civic life because ultimately, the goal of education is a transformative one and they'll need these skills to challenge long-held assumptions that keep things status quo.

Nonetheless, the relatively small number of responses that referenced the relationship between literacy, power, and civic engagement concerned me. Without a guiding set of principles for literacy instruction that explicitly wrestle with these issues, it is very difficult to strive toward critical civic empathy in practice; indeed, it is startlingly easy to revert to strategies that reinforce narrow neoliberal ideologies of literacy. In reality, it is a struggle to embody these commitments even when these principles are in place, as conversations with Jerica Coffey and Ashley Englander, the focus teachers from Chapter 1, demonstrate. Let's turn now to a consideration of the complex relationship they experienced between beliefs and practice, in order to demonstrate the vigilance we must always maintain in order to pursue democratic aims in our teaching.

TAKING A PRAGMATIC APPROACH TO FOSTERING CRITICAL CIVIC EMPATHY

Chapter 1 detailed the ways in which two high school English teachers sought to connect the study of literature to broader goals of civic empowerment and agency for their students. I return to them now because further conversations between us revealed the constant reflection that they engaged in as they tried to act on their beliefs within school structures that seemed designed to thwart them at every turn. Their reflections demonstrate the sense of pragmatism necessary to teach toward critical civic empathy—the acknowledgment of inherent tensions and halting progress that characterize this endeavor. Their strategies can help us all as we negotiate our own contexts and contradictions.

During the semester that I observed Jerica's and Ashley's classrooms, I met with them periodically to discuss what I was seeing and ensure that my findings accurately represented the intentions of both teachers. We also engaged in dialogue about the successes and challenges of approaching literacy with a focus on equity, democracy, and justice. In one meeting, I provided the teachers with a handout (see Appendix G) containing brief snippets of text from *Literacy: Reading the Word and the World* that described what Freire and Macedo (1987) considered four traditional approaches to reading and literacy—academic, utilitarian, cognitive, and romantic. Each of these approaches presented different purposes for literacy, from acquiring knowledge of "great works" to functioning in contemporary society to achieving personal fulfillment. I then juxtaposed these snippets with Freire and Macedo's description of "emancipatory literacy" and quotes from Henry Giroux and Theresa Perry that provided some language for teachers to chew on about the relationship of literacy to freedom. After spending some time discussing the merits and drawbacks of traditional approaches to literacy, I steered the conversation toward an analysis of what emancipatory literacy meant to each of them.

Ashley began by saying, "No matter how engaged my room can feel—how caring—I still feel like this emancipatory thing is a bit elusive for me." Her statement triggered recognition in Jerica about the difficulty of measuring success when it comes to raising students' consciousness about society. She responded, "In a society like the one we live in, it's going to be a lifelong struggle to liberate ourselves." She then articulated what she believed to qualify as success for instruction oriented toward liberation: "If we're raising their consciousness about the way that they are oppressed in our society and the way that oppression works, and then what struggle against that looks like, and how their communities have struggled, I would say that's what the emancipatory approach is."

In this case, Jerica defined success as understanding oppression and strategies for community resistance. She referred to the traditional approaches to reading, dismissing them as possible models for powerful English instruction; as she claimed, "None of this is about freedom, and literacy as a practice of freedom." Ashley quickly agreed, "They're more about different ways to approach the act of reading as opposed to the purpose of reading." In this case, both teachers characterized emancipatory literacy as providing an appropriate guiding philosophy for literacy instruction based in student social empowerment.

When I gave them the opportunity to review fieldnotes from my previous classroom observations, they began reflecting on the ways that their beliefs about emancipatory literacy translated (or failed to translate) into their practice. I asked them to explain what they noticed when reflecting upon particular class sessions, and they quickly zeroed in on the moments when they saw themselves deviating from their professed beliefs; in fact, they were often quite critical of their own perceived shortcomings and slow to acknowledge their strengths. Although the teachers initially criticized themselves, the conversations that arose from these reflections on classroom moments eventually revealed systemic barriers to critical literacy pedagogy that teachers constantly strive to mitigate in pragmatic ways; namely, grading and test preparation.

For instance, as Ashley read a fieldnote describing a class session in which her students reviewed vocabulary words and performed poetry for their peers, she shook her head and exclaimed:

This illuminates why there is a sense of patchiness for my students about purpose. I'm doing a lot of, "C'mon guys, this is important for your grade." I'm telling them why they should be feeling this is important, and it's clearly because I'm panicking that they don't think this is important or they don't have the same stake in their grade that I do.

Though critical of her practice, Ashley located the root of her preoccupation with grades in the school system itself; she stated, "I think it's something that's been normalized for me through the school environment over the years." She lamented the fact that she had not been given opportunities to connect grading in any meaningful way with the literacy goals she had for her students—with, as she put it, "the values that I care about."

Nevertheless, she constantly sought to find ways to reconcile an arbitrary grading system with authentic learning outcomes. One effort aimed at accomplishing this goal was her decision to make classroom participation the largest percentage of students' grades in order to emphasize its importance. She explained her rationale: "Mostly it's because I started realizing that someone could be learning, growing, and contributing without turning in a lot of work. I needed a grading scale that would reflect that." Ashley expressed a deep commitment to the idea of grades as tools that students could use to measure personal growth in their learning and that meant more to them than, as she put it, "Am I passing or am I failing? Am I the best or am I the worst?"

Just after Ashley explained what happened in her classroom to the other teachers during the group meeting, Jerica reassured her that she was dealing with similar issues. Jerica pointed to the fieldnote that she was examining about her own practice and said, "I say some really messed up things." She directed everyone's attention to a moment described in the fieldnote when she reprimanded students who had not turned in an essay assignment by saying, "Half of you haven't turned in your essays, and that means half of you aren't doing well in this class. You need to turn that in." She turned back to us and asked, "Where's my messaging? How am I humanizing them if I'm starting off with that?" Jerica shared Ashley's concern that grading systems stand opposed to the process of consciousness-raising that they saw as key to emancipatory literacy.

Jerica also critiqued herself for losing her sense of purpose when she engaged in standardized test preparation with her students. While she often attempted to transform test preparation into meaningful instruction by making multiple-choice questions out of the material they were studying, she sometimes found herself engaging in straightforward test drills. As the California Standards Test (CST) in ELA approached in the spring, Jerica began referring to it with urgency. When the test was a week-and-a-half away, she told students: "We have to make sure that everyone does well on the CST." She later reiterated her statement and appealed to students, "I need you all to shine on this test we're about to take." She told students that they needed to do well so that "when you apply to colleges and they see that you went to this school, they'll say, dang, that's a good school." When she read her words during our conversation, Jerica groaned and looked guiltily at us. She exclaimed in dismay, "The purpose that I say is that you have to succeed on the CST next week!" Ashley shared a knowing laugh with her.

Keep in mind that these same educators who were critiquing themselves so harshly also were doing innovative and (in my mind) transformative work with their students. I think that the tendency toward self-criticism exhibited by Jerica and Ashley speaks to the way that teachers concentrate on their own efforts and are sometimes hesitant to consider structural factors for fear of seeming like they are making excuses or abnegating their responsibility for student success. But I see it as actually quite the contrary—I suggest that part of the reason that they could develop such powerful pedagogy that helped foster the development of critical civic empathy was because they were willing to engage in sustained reflection about their practice and find ways to move forward through the inevitable roadblocks and contradictions that come from working within schools and a society struggling with structural inequities. Pragmatism does not imply simply giving in to the elements of schooling that dampen possibilities for mutual humanization and social action; nor does it involve rejecting institutions to the point where we negate them altogether. Instead, it involves a continuous process of inquiry and consciousness-raising in which we interrogate our practice, find opportunities for small moves, and celebrate incremental progress.

This work requires support. Both Jerica and Ashley benefited from professional networks that offered them encouragement and resources to continue their development as teachers. Yet they did not restrict their learning and engagement to their professional lives; they also engaged in civic activities outside of their teaching that built upon and expanded the commitments they sought to embody with their students. While I have long believed that teachers' personal civic participation influences their classroom practice, I was able to support this belief only anecdotally until recently, when I was able to participate in a second survey that provided more empirical support. I explore these results next.

COMMITMENTS TO DEMOCRACY INSIDE AND OUTSIDE THE CLASSROOM

The Inequality Project is a research endeavor spearheaded by John Rogers and Joel Westheimer that explores what students learn about economic inequality from their high school teachers, and how teacher practice is related to political ideology and civic engagement. Because Rogers and Westheimer view civic learning as the purview of all teachers—not just those in the discipline of social studies—they include English teachers as respondents in the surveys they design and conduct across the United States and Canada.

During the spring of 2015, the Inequality Project conducted an online survey of more than 2,000 high school teachers focused on teaching about economic inequality. Though detailing all of the survey findings is beyond the scope of this chapter (you can learn more at Rogers & Westheimer, 2017), I focus here on one result that merits particular attention, considering the theme of this chapter—the relationship between teacher civic engagement and civic teaching practice.

The survey asked teachers to report the nature and frequency of their civic engagement based on how often in the past month they followed the news, talked about politics or government, and/or participated in an organization that tries to make a difference in their community. Among the 548 English teacher respondents, 27% were characterized as minimally engaged (engaging in activities never or once), 51% were moderately engaged (engaging weekly), and 22% were highly engaged (engaging a few times per week to daily).

Teachers also were asked how often they facilitated discussions about social and political issues with their students. Only 1% of English teacher respondents said that they never facilitated discussions, while the majority (58%) reported facilitating discussions at least once per week. This finding alone was important because it demonstrated that English teachers should be taken seriously as civic educators, considering the frequency with which they are talking about civic issues with their students.

But what was most fascinating was the relationship between these two variables. Findings indicated that teachers who were more civically engaged facilitated discussions about social and political issues more frequently. Now, while facilitating discussions about current events does not necessarily imply that teachers are embracing critical orientations toward literacy and considering empathy in a civic sense, I would suggest that it is a step in the right direction. It is impossible to cultivate critical civic empathy in students without being civically knowledgeable and engaged oneself, so it makes sense that teachers are better prepared to foster this disposition when they participate in public life. Such participation has the potential to introduce us to our fellow citizens, engage us in productive problem solving, and broaden our ideological horizons. Plus, it awakens us to ideas and resources that we can bring into our classrooms to add nuance and complexity to our pedagogy.

I believe that this finding should influence the way we think about teacher education and professional development. What if opportunities for civic engagement were built into preservice preparation programs? What if we spent more time during professional development sessions forging connections with local community organizations and studying how to talk with students productively about sensitive and controversial topics? If we want our students to be able to tackle the challenges of the 21st century and beyond with discernment and empathy, we need to be willing and prepared to embrace little-p politics and welcome the messiness of democratic life into the classroom. Even if you are not in a position to benefit from or create large-scale efforts, you can still gather together with like-minded colleagues—as Jerica and Ashley did with me—and share ideas to spur your thinking and keep you motivated.

For instance, during our conversations, both teachers strategized about ways to engage students in authentic forms of assessment that would involve the students in their local communities. Ashley discussed using the novel *The Hunger Games* as a catalyst for action research about "the role of government in society and its ability to grant or deny access to resources." Jerica suggested connecting students with community organizations that are working to influence local and state policy, in order to show them that "organizing is the only way that change ever comes about." Ashley pounced upon this idea and talked excitedly about developing community asset maps to show students the wealth of resources available around them. As the teachers talked, more and more possibilities emerged and barriers seemed—at least temporarily—to fade away. The teachers' conversations strove to embody what researcher Susan Lytle and her colleagues (Lytle, Portnoy, Waff, & Buckley, 2009) call the defining characteristic of teacher research, namely, "its primary commitment to improving the life chances of urban students and schools in a complex, embattled, and continually restructuring system . . . through a critical social and political analysis of the educational system at many levels" (p. 40).

There are also steps that you can take personally to develop dispositions toward critical civic empathy, even with limited time and resources. First, pose this question to yourself: To what extent do I consider myself informed about local, national, and global events? If you are dissatisfied with your answer, evaluate the steps you can take to gain a diverse set of perspectives on issues that matter to you and your students. Reach beyond mainstream news sources to explore a range of media platforms—I suggest youth-produced media content from sites such as Youth Radio (youthradio.org/), the Black Youth Project (blackyouthproject.com/), and Youth Voices (www.youthvoices.live/). One of the necessary components of mutual humanization is contact with various individuals and perspectives; as we've explored, such contact can occur through engagement with stories as well as interaction with individuals.

Second, as overwhelming as teaching responsibilities can be, seek to identify your civic passions and find organizations with which you can engage inside and outside the classroom. Teaching is an act of civic engagement itself, but the struggle for equity and justice requires our participation as private citizens as well. Often, we do not need to look far beyond our professional networks to connect with others interested in social action; many teacher organizations and grassroots educator groups pop up in local communities in order to advocate for public causes that impact schools and communities. The New York Coalition of Radical Educators (NYCoRE) and the Association of Raza Educators (ARE) are two such organizations that I have been fortunate to learn from. More suggestions for taking first steps to action are offered in the Conclusion to this book.

If we hope to help our students develop commitments to critical civic empathy, we first need to nourish our own civic identities—both for our own benefit and for the insights that such participation will give us into new potential classroom project ideas. In order to exercise the muscle of empathy, we must welcome the public sphere into both our personal and professional lives.

CONCLUSION

As teachers, we are accustomed to constantly moving forward. The next class is always on the way in and the next school day is always here before we know it. Our focus is (rightly) trained on our students as we search for instructional strategies, resources, and opportunities we can share with them. Amid this whirlwind, we do not often find the opportunity to stop and consider how we are nourishing the most crucial student resource— ourselves. You likely obtained this book in order to learn new ideas for educating toward empathy; I hope that one idea that sticks with you is that these ideas will come to fruition in the classroom only if you nurture your-self as a citizen and embrace teaching as a political act. As all-consuming as teaching can be—and as much as teaching is already a profound form of civic engagement—we need to educate ourselves about the most pressing issues of the day and involve ourselves in political life as public intellectuals.

Though the grind of daily classroom life and the contradictory pressures facing public education writ large inevitably will cause us to lose our way at times (and tempt us to blame ourselves when things go off track), we must work continuously to name a purpose for literacy education that stands against inequity and for the full blossoming of democratic life. And then we must act pragmatically upon that purpose both inside and outside the classroom as role models for our students of what engaged citizens do to the best of our abilities.

DISCUSSION/REFLECTION QUESTIONS
1. What have your experiences (or fears) been with the idea of allowing politics into the classroom? How do colleagues at your school respond when students bring up controversial social issues?
2. How do you conceptualize the purpose(s) of literacy education? What do you see as the relationship between your purpose and your practice? What changes would you like to make?
3. How would you characterize your level of civic engagement outside of the classroom? What relationship do you see between your civic engagement and your teaching practice?

Conclusion

This book has aimed to disrupt popular understandings of empathy in society, offer critical civic empathy as a guiding principle for English education in a polarized political context, and present literacy practices that can help bring this democratic disposition to life in classroom and community learning contexts. These chapters have provided a window into the sustained planning, action, and reflection necessary to swim against the tide that seeks to reduce education to a set of isolated academic skills and instead embrace a vision of literacy that prepares students to tackle the challenges of the 21st century and beyond with consciousness, compassion, and commitment to equity and justice.

Fostering the development of critical civic empathy in ourselves and our students does not require abandoning or supplementing the practices of our discipline; instead, I have endeavored to demonstrate how the foundational activities of literary analysis, classroom discussion, research, and multimodal composition can be transformed into opportunities for encouraging mutual humanization and community social action. And I have emphasized the need for teachers to continuously analyze their own identities, civic behaviors, and philosophies of literacy education as they develop curriculum and pedagogy.

Over the course of the year it took to write this book, I felt as if I possessed a special radar for noticing every time the word *empathy* was uttered, either in passing by a political pundit or in the context of longer think pieces about the state of U.S. civic life. And the term was everywhere. It was raised quite a bit in the context of the current presidential administration—arguments have raged about which groups of citizens deserve empathy, which groups receive it, and why it seems to be in a state of continual freefall. While I have been tempted to catalog and discuss these instances, I ultimately made the decision not to, both because the constant stream of news inevitably will make any of my attempts at analysis immediately outdated and also because I am invested in advocating for the cultivation of justice-oriented teaching commitments that can adapt to any of the challenges that will arise in the coming decades that we cannot even imagine yet.

In this spirit, I conclude the book by considering some of the enduring tensions that teachers who seek to educate in the spirit of critical civic empathy likely will face in the course of their efforts. Though I promise no definitive resolutions to these tensions, I believe that anticipating them and understanding where they come from can better prepare us to manage them and prevent us from being thrown off course.

I first note the limits of empathy in order to counter the naïve idea that identifying with the experiences and perspectives of others is sufficient to fulfill our duties as citizens. I will then explore the actions that must accompany our dispositions in order to sustain a movement for educational and social justice. Finally, I encourage us to look forward and imagine the democracy we continually strive to bring into existence through our work educating future generations of citizens.

THE LIMITS OF EMPATHY

I will be the first to acknowledge that empathy is not the magic bullet for countering divisiveness and polarization in U.S. society and that any usefulness that it does possess matters little if it does not inspire civic action. Indeed, if the empathy that we develop does not influence our behavior at the ballot box or on the streets of our communities, then the disposition actually does not mean much at all. This is the most obvious limitation of empathy—the fact that it does not have a demonstrated causal relationship to sustained differences in behavior (Prinz, 2014). We soon will discuss the steps needed to make the necessary moves from empathy to action, but first I want to address some tensions that emerge even in the fostering of empathy itself: (1) whether some individuals or ideas do not deserve empathy in the first place; and (2) how to manage the ethics of asking students to empathize with people from groups to which they themselves do not belong.

First, as discussed in Chapter 2, welcoming all perspectives into the classroom in the name of intellectual exchange and perspective-taking is not necessarily the way to foster critical civic empathy, particularly when the discussions engage with core elements of individuals' identities; in fact, this openness actually can do the opposite by jeopardizing the emotional (and sometimes literal) safety of young people and creating a hostile atmosphere for dialogue. Particularly now, at a moment when hate speech has become a renewed topic of national conversation, we teachers need to ask ourselves: What views do not deserve empathy and will not be permitted in our classrooms?

We need to be prepared as teachers to frame the parameters of discussions in our classrooms and be very clear about those parameters with our students. I spend a great deal of time at the beginning of every school year setting norms for discussion, which I then return to with my classes each time we engage with controversial civic issues. Also, returning to Chapter 5, we need to make (little-p) political choices about what it means to embrace values of equity and justice in our classrooms, and take steps to ensure that our classrooms are humanizing spaces for young people from minoritized communities. This may mean framing issues for discussion in ways that preclude the possibility of introducing opinions that denigrate an individual's or a group's identity (even when masked as political positions). Helping students understand these distinctions is a time-consuming and delicate process, but one that is at the heart of truly engaging with and fostering critical civic empathy.

The second issue involves consideration of the identity groups to which we and our students belong and the ways that these memberships influence how and why we approach empathy in the classroom. We are much more likely to feel empathy for in-group members; that is, people who belong to the our own race, class, gender, religious affiliaton, and so on. The reasons are relatively simple—for each identity that we have in common with someone else, the shorter the imaginative leap to understand the other person's experiences and perspectives because we likely share some of them in common. Feeling empathy for out-group members requires us to gain more knowledge about them and step more completely outside of our own frames of reference. Understanding your sources of knowledge (and blind spots) as well as those of your students is an important step toward crafting a meaningful approach to critical civic empathy. Are you teaching in a segregated school in which many of your students belong to similar identity groups? Are you teaching in a heterogeneous context with many layers of difference to manage? Do you belong to similar or different identity groups than your students?

When we do not consider these questions and prepare ourselves with the knowledge we need in order to foster authentic connections, we often take a reductive approach to bridging divides by simply focusing on our common humanity. You may be Black and I may be White, but we are all humans underneath it all, right? Decades of scholarship from feminists of color (Delgado-Bernal, 1998; hooks, 1994) have explored the ways that these default expressions of identity consistently revert to White, cis-gender, heterosexual, patriarchal Christian norms and marginalize the experiences of young people from minoritized communities. They also place emotional burdens on members of minoritized communities to explain their humanity to others in ways that members of majority communities largely are not asked to do.

These burdens can amount to micro-aggressions that take physical and mental health tolls on those who repeatedly must share their counter-stories. In many ways, members of minoritized communities have long had to possess empathy (or at the very least perspective-taking) for majority communities simply in order to navigate society and figure out ways to survive, whereas members of majority communities have enjoyed a choice about whether and how to engage in this behavior. As teachers, we must think about the ways that the political work is different depending on whether it is related to majority or minoritized groups of students. Members of majority groups need multiple, meaningful, and sustained opportunities to deconstruct their own privileges and get to know individuals from groups other than their own. Simply reading a text or two by an author is not enough and actually can end up reinforcing rather than breaking down stereotypes. Members of minoritized groups need opportunities to process and share experiences of marginalization or oppression and understand that they are not being asked to empathize with those who question their humanity; instead, they need opportunities to forge solidarity, bring their concerns into the public sphere to be taken seriously, and strategize about how to respond to those seeking to dehumanize them in public life.

For those teachers who might be nervous about how to empathize with students whose identities differ from their own, researcher Chezare Warren (2015) has been exploring the successes and challenges of cross-racial and cross-cultural empathy, particularly with White female teachers seeking to empathize with students of color. He highlights the need for teachers to listen to students and adopt students' social and cultural perspectives in order to interrogate their own instruction and make it more culturally sustaining. The key here is humility and an openness to change, along with a commitment to continually adding to our cultural repertoires by seeking out new perspectives in print and in person. Let's turn now to some suggestions for ways to get started.

EMPATHY INTO ACTION

In order to avoid falling into the trap of promoting action-less empathy with our students, I suggest that we consider ways that we can make commitments to progress in three interrelated areas of our lives: the personal, the professional, and the civic. Chapter 5 provided a roadmap for assessing our beliefs about our discipline and our levels of civic engagement; once we have begun that self-assessment, we are prepared to consider actions we may want to take to bolster the development of critical civic empathy in ourselves—a development that will then translate into practice in the classroom.

I won't spend much time on tips for cultivating empathy in personal life because everyone is negotiating different contexts and has different needs and goals. I will, however, generally advocate for the continuous seeking out of new people and new perspectives in any form that this process may take for you. The success of social movements that aim to expand the rights of minoritized groups consistently involves attempts to reach hearts and minds; to show people that those demanding change are not cynical political operatives but family members, neighbors, and coworkers—people they know and love. The more that we welcome opportunities into our lives to meet people who differ from us and to engage in sustained contact with them, the more likely that our capacities for empathy will grow.

In terms of professional life, a wealth of resources exists that can make the journey toward fostering empathy in the classroom less daunting and more collaborative. I recommend a few strategies that have helped me figure out where to start.

Join National and Community-Based Professional Organizations

As discussed throughout this book, empathy is a topic of interest across the educational community; this means that it is definitely on the radar of the major national literacy teacher organizations, including NWP, NCTE, and ILA. The benefits of membership in professional organizations are many, but one of the most rewarding is access to colleagues who share ideas that you can integrate into your classroom immediately and in the longer term throughout all the twists and turns your career may take. NWP's Educator Innovator network engages in national campaigns related to connected learning and civic engagement and regularly offers grants to educators who are making innovative learning opportunities available to students during and after the school day. NCTE publishes a range of journals sharing the latest research and practice aimed at students from kindergartners to pre- and inservice teachers and encourages members to join commissions and standing committees that wrestle with topics including citizenship, the school-to-prison pipeline, and social justice advocacy.

It is through these organizations that I bolster my knowledge and skills about critical community literacies. For instance, the July 2016 issue of NCTE's *English Education* journal, edited by Marcelle Haddix and Yolanda Sealey-Ruiz, centered on Black girls' literacies in calling for more responsive literacy pedagogy. Other professional journals have helped advance my thinking about integrating ethnic studies into literacy education (de los Rios, 2017), leveraging the linguistic resources of Black and Latinx students (Martinez, 2017), and embracing hip-hop literacies to analyze language and society (Kelly, 2013).

These national organizations often sponsor local affiliates in which you can participate throughout the year; in addition, a little digging often will turn up community-based groups of educators gathering to build solidarity, write curriculum, and share resources.

Network on Social Media

Whenever I read insightful articles or listen to powerful interviews on the topics of critical literacy, civic engagement, or empathy, I immediately search for the authors and creators on Twitter; reading their tweets then introduces me to more thinkers and more resources in a snowball effect that helps me develop an online professional learning network. Twitter now boasts a huge educator presence, and I can say with confidence that I collect links to more resources from this platform than from almost any other source.

Almost every week you can plug into Twitter chats engaging with issues of equity and educational justice, from #educolor to #hiphoped, to connect with educators near and far offering inspiration, sharing challenges, and building community.

Connect with Any and All Who Are Willing and Committed

My professional life has taken me across the country and back, to cities from New York and Boston to Los Angeles and El Paso, Texas. In every community I have lived, I have spent a great deal of time getting to know its residents and asking them about the businesses, schools, museums, parks, community centers, restaurants, houses of worship, and other landmarks that matter to them as sources of community cultural wealth. Schools are crucial educational institutions, but a misguided belief that they are the *only* educational institutions in a community runs counter to the pursuit and practice of critical civic empathy. Allies and fellow educators abound if you take the time to look and build the trust necessary to ask for support—you can even engage your students in the practice of community asset mapping to bring these resources into focus.

These practices can offer us the sustenance and fire needed to bring a commitment to empathy to the challenges facing our schools and society now and into the future. Yet, although our attention is rightly trained for the most part on our classrooms, we also must expand our focus outward and advocate as educators and citizens for educational policies that align with our equity-oriented vision. One step toward imbuing literacy education with a stronger civic purpose and connecting students' reading, writing, listening, and speaking skills to the ability to participate effectively in a democratic society is a thorough re-evaluation of the explicit and implicit goals expressed in policy documents about literacy and civic education. In this spirit, I want to offer some big-picture considerations for moving the field forward that we cannot accomplish single-handedly but can begin promoting throughout the educational landscape.

Bringing educational policy in line with a more socially just and democratic vision requires several major changes. First, testing must be utilized more judiciously as a means of providing teachers with data to inform their instruction rather than as an ultimate measure of student learning and teacher success. Across all of the projects in which I have been involved, teachers have told me that high-stakes testing negatively impacted their ability to implement civic learning opportunities and other forms of instruction into their classes, and that the frenzy caused by looming sanctions forced them to spend many days and weeks on test preparation rather than meaningful literacy practices. In addition to reducing the stakes of standardized tests, the field would be improved by the development of formative, performance-based assessments that allow students to demonstrate growth and mastery of skills through engagement in authentic activities. Such a change would elevate examples of civic learning, like the letters that Jerica's students wrote to the governor, as forms of assessment as respected and encouraged as any exam—and indeed, more so.

Considering the rich learning that emerged whenever the teachers with whom I have worked had the opportunity to dialogue with one another, I advocate for the development of professional development communities that prioritize practitioner inquiry. Such communities of practice encourage dialogue between teachers and situate them as public intellectuals and instructional leaders. Basing professional development in problems of practice within teachers' classrooms instead of offering one-size-fits-all prescriptions honors the complexity of the classroom environment and supports democratic relationships within the school building between administrators and teachers and between teachers and students.

English teachers in particular need instruction that helps them understand the role that language and literacy have played historically both in maintaining institutional and social inequality and also in supporting struggles for justice and freedom. The teachers in my life developed sophisticated social and cultural analyses through powerful educational experiences in fields like ethnic studies and critical theory; exposing all teachers to such experiences has the potential to encourage reflection that can influence teachers' philosophies and pedagogies. Apprentice teachers should be given opportunities to reflect on the experiences and attitudes that they bring to the classroom and to develop goals for their instruction that go beyond success on standardized assessments. They also should be guided to develop relationships with members of the communities in which they will be teaching. All of the teachers represented in this book tailored their instruction to maximize the resources that students' communities offered, which engaged students and contributed to making their pedagogy more civic-oriented.

Finally, civic education policy should refocus its attention on teachers across all subject areas rather than maintaining a strict allegiance to history teachers alone. Civic education standards and curriculum often are situated within history departments, sending the message that all other teachers do not share responsibility for providing students with the knowledge, skills, and attitudes to participate in public life. The teachers profiled throughout this book provide strong evidence that the discipline of English language arts is uniquely positioned to explore the democratic power of language and literacy, and they need support to take the field in that direction.

FACING THE 21ST CENTURY (AND BEYOND)

As discussed in Chapter 4, the signifier *21st century* has become ubiquitous in educational policy discourse. A glance at most local, state, and national education plans reveals reference after reference to the need for "21st-century schools" focusing on "21st-century skills" that prepare "21st-century students."

But what exactly does it mean to live and learn in the 21st century? And, more important, how should we conceptualize and implement the term in classroom practice? I think that the *21st-century* modifier requires a high level of specificity, considering the huge amounts of spending on infrastructure, curriculum, and professional development that it is inspiring across the country. Though the meaning of a phrase that dictates so much investment should be clear, I fear that it is not. Instead, teachers encounter a fuzzy definition based on the premise that the flow of information enabled by digital technology and the interconnectedness of the global economy mean that we should use devices in the classroom and encourage project-based learning.

Education policymakers and practitioners continue to use the term in an aspirational way when it comes to learning as if we are not currently *living in* the 21st century—a situation that ignores social and educational realities and renders the term an empty signifier. Yet I bring it up because I want to call attention to what I believe is unique and urgent about this time we find ourselves in; namely, the possibilities for expanded communication and connection coexisting with the narrow tribalist and populist ideologies proliferating around the globe. We live in contradictory times in which digital media offer avenues for more voices than ever to join democratic dialogues, but are used more often to foster isolation and polarization. We are experiencing new iterations of social movements fighting for equity around race, gender, and immigration status at the same time that overtly racist speech is coming out of the shadows, and social and political inequities continue to structure public life. Our 21st-century democracy faces unprecedented challenges that call for creative solutions—ones that I hope can be born through the fostering of critical civic empathy.

Yet while these challenges may be unprecedented, the struggle itself has been waged for as long as this country has existed. I recently re-read Martin Luther King, Jr.'s, "I've Been to the Mountaintop" speech—the last one he delivered before he was assassinated in 1968—and I was struck by the continued relevance and power of his words:

The nation is sick. Trouble is in the land; confusion all around. . . . But I know, somehow, that only when it is dark enough can you see the stars. And I see God working in this period of the twentieth century in a way that men, in some strange way, are responding. Something is happening in our world. The masses of people are rising up. And wherever they are assembled today, whether they are in Johannesburg, South Africa; Nairobi, Kenya; Accra, Ghana; New York City; Atlanta, Georgia; Jackson, Mississippi; or Memphis, Tennessee—the cry is always the same: "We want to be free."

I think that a meditation on these words is an appropriate way to end this book because Dr. King's legacy is so often oversimplified and distorted when it comes to considerations of empathy. He is remembered for his dream (1963)—for the harmonious image of "little black boys and black girls holding hands with little white boys and white girls as sisters and brothers"—and is almost universally admired today for his messages of nonviolence and compassion. What is not as often remembered is that Dr. King was held in contempt by many White Americans at the time of his death because of his work denouncing the forces of White supremacy that structured urban poverty and housing discrimination. He not only called for peace—he also called for economic boycotts and campaigns against voter suppression.

If we remember only the elements of Dr. King's message about tolerance and character, we fall into the trap of individual empathy. We easily can be lulled into a false sense of righteousness in which we fail to interrogate the complicity we may have in maintaining structural inequity or take the steps necessary to translate commitments to mutual humanization into justice-oriented social action. The work of embodying empathy in everyday democratic life is not always harmonious; indeed, it is often wrenching, exhausting, and thankless. Yet Dr. King reminds us that just as people rose up in the 20th century, we must continue to do so in the 21st century in order to foster in our children the love of justice that will bring the next generation to the next mountaintop and continue the beautiful struggle for freedom.

Civically Engaged Unit Planning Template

Essential Question(s)/Enduring Understanding(s):
Common Core Standard(s): ☐ Reading ☐ Writing ☐ Speaking/Listening ☐ Language
Civic Engagement Focus:
Summative Assessment(s): ☐ Real-World Topics ☐ Civic Dialogue ☐ Authentic Audience ☐ Community Action
Text Set: ☐ Fiction (novels, short stories, poems, drama) ☐ Nonfiction (newspaper/magazine/blog articles, speeches, informational texts) ☐ Multimedia (film clips, online content, podcasts) ☐ Authors (diversity of gender, race, age, country of origin, ability status, sexual orientation)
What do students need to know and be able to do in order to successfully complete the summative assessment?

Content	Skills

Classroom Activities (Begin daily lesson planning on back)

Template for Learning How to "Flow" in Debate

Sample Silly Resolution: Resolved: Dogs are better pets than cats.

Affirmative team—Thinks dogs are better pets

Negative team—Thinks cats are better pets

1st Aff	1st Neg	2nd Aff	2nd Neg
[1st reason dogs are better pets]	[Refute!]	[Support!]	[Refute!]
[2nd reason dogs are better pets]	[Refute!]	[Support!]	[Refute!]
[3rd reason dogs are better pets]	[Refute!]	[Support!]	[Refute!]
	[1st reason cats are better pets]	[Refute!]	[Support!]
	[2nd reason cats are better pets]	[Refute!]	[Support!]
	[3rd reason cats are better pets]	[Refute!]	[Support!]

YPAR Research Proposal Template

RESEARCH STUDY: (give it a title of your own)

Community Tour

It's Friday afternoon, and I'm going to take you on a tour of my community . . .

Research Topic

My research will be on the topic of _____.
I chose this topic because . . .

Research Question

My question is: _____

Quality of My Research

My research is meaningful to me because . . .
My research is specific because . . .
My research is data-driven because . . .

Review of Research

Social reproduction/resistance theory [the theories we studied in class] argue that . . .

Methods

Survey, photovoice, interviews

Findings and Analysis

Brief Introductions to YPAR Data Collection Strategies

Existing Information

You can learn about school conditions from a number of public sources. Newspapers, for example, can be searched for recent articles about problems facing local schools. Government websites feature data, reports, and legislation. To meet federal guidelines, the state and local districts must create annual reports on their programs and student performance. You can access much of this information online, through general searches and by browsing the web pages. It is often helpful to use these data sources to compare conditions in wealthy and low-income communities.

Of course, public reports don't have a critical point of view. They often lack vital information and they frequently downplay or disguise inequalities. You should always ask: "Do these data make sense from my own experience?" "What is not being reported here?" By identifying gaps in existing data, you can create your own research.

Interviews

Interviews are very challenging interactions and you can learn a lot from them about how different people think about important issues. They are also fun. You can interview other students, parents, community members, educators, policymakers, and activists. Interviews with young people document the daily experiences of youth and how they make sense of these experiences. Interviews with educators, policymakers, and activists provide student researchers with a record of adults explaining why things are the way they are and how they might be changed.

There are some obvious "handy hints" for good interviews: plan well, know what you want to learn, design good questions, practice or role-play the interview, have alternate follow-up questions, allow sufficient "wait-time," make sure your tape recorder has batteries and you know how to work it, research the interviewee's background when you can, and work with a partner so one can concentrate on questions while the other takes notes.

117

Focus Groups

Focus groups is the term that researchers use for group interviews. There are many ways to run a focus group, such as small breakout groups or large-group discussions; and there are a variety of ways to get the discussions going, such as direct questions to individuals, turn-taking answers, or more of a free-flowing discussion that is guided, but not strongly controlled, by the researcher. You can supply various materials, such as information that the group might not be familiar with, charts or videos, or simply questions.

Focus groups are not just a more "efficient" way to get information from several people at one time. Focus groups add a group dynamic that influences the responses people give. Whether that influence is helpful, and whether it adds to or hides the expression and meaning of individual responses, depend on how the group is "managed." Focus groups allow you to see how people come to a consensus, how they go through a change in their thinking when new ideas or vocabulary is introduced, and how they disagree. Focus groups can be followed up with individual interviews.

Surveys

A survey asks a set of common questions to a large number of individuals. Some surveys seek responses from students in a classroom or school. Other surveys seek responses from youth in public places such as parks or malls.

Surveys can range from a few questions to a great many questions; however, shorter surveys tend to draw a more focused response. It is important to design surveys that maintain the same measurement for responses. In other words, you might design a survey to measure responses on a scale of 1–5, with 1 representing a response of "never" and 5 representing a response of "always." Likewise, you might decide to simplify a survey's response options by offering informants only "yes" or "no" response options. All surveys must be "field-tested." That is, the survey should be given to a few "trial" survey-takers in circumstances similar to those in which the real survey will be given. Asking yourself a few questions after the trials can lead to beneficial revisions: Do people seem interested in or bored with answering all the questions? Does anyone get stuck on a question or misunderstand the meaning?

Fieldnotes

Fieldnotes are the researcher's diary or journal of data collection activities. Fieldnotes are an important part of the research process because they record what you see and what you are thinking. Fieldnotes typically are kept in a notebook, with each entry recording the date, time, and location of the activity. When first taken, notes are typically brief and fragmented, and may be illegible. A crucial step can be to "write up" the notes—completing partial thoughts, adding unrecorded circumstances, and so on. This write-up step needs structured and perhaps supervised time to complete. The objective of the fieldnotes is to record what you see and hear. No detail should be considered unimportant; no incident too small to record.

You also should create a section in each entry for "observer comments." This is the space for you to reflect on questions such as: "Why did the teacher focus on that one student?" "Why aren't these students angrier about what they have experienced?" "How does this classroom differ from the one we observed last week?" "How might I have asked that question differently?"

YPAR Student Survey Model

11th-Grade School Survey

The junior class is completing a research project about issues in our school and community that matter to us. We created this survey and want to know how every student in the school feels about the issues we are researching. When we get these surveys back from all of the students at Animo Watts, we will learn about how our community really feels and it will help us to think about how to make our school and community better. This survey is anonymous, so no one will know what your responses are. It is very important that you are honest so that we get true responses to analyze. Thank you for your help! We will share the results with you when we are done.

	PLEASE CIRCLE ONLY ONE RESPONSE!	Strongly Disagree	Disagree	Agree	Strongly Agree
1	I feel safe walking down the street in my community.	1	2	3	4
2	I have been approached about joining a gang.	1	2	3	4
3	At least one person who is close to me is a gang member.	1	2	3	4
4	I have been the victim of a violent crime in my community.	1	2	3	4
5	At least one person who is close to me has been the victim of a violent crime in my community.	1	2	3	4
6	I feel that gang members control my community.	1	2	3	4
7	I feel pride in my community.	1	2	3	4
8	Education is important to me.	1	2	3	4
9	I am worried that I will not graduate from high school.	1	2	3	4
10	I feel that this school is preparing me for college.	1	2	3	4
11	At least one person who is close to me has dropped out of high school.	1	2	3	4
12	I am scared that I will be a failure in life.	1	2	3	4
13	I have used illegal drugs at least once in the past 6 months.	1	2	3	4

	PLEASE CIRCLE ONLY ONE RESPONSE!	Strongly Disagree	Disagree	Agree	Strongly Agree
14	I have used alcohol at least once in the past 6 months.	1	2	3	4
15	At least one person who is close to me has used illegal drugs at least once in the past month.	1	2	3	4
16	I know someone I could buy illegal drugs from if I wanted to.	1	2	3	4
17	I have been pressured by a friend to use illegal drugs.	1	2	3	4
18	I have had sexual intercourse at least once in the past 6 months.	1	2	3	4
19	I use protection (or plan to use protection) each time I have sexual intercourse.	1	2	3	4
20	I know at least one teenage girl who is or has been pregnant.	1	2	3	4
21	I know at least one teenage dad.	1	2	3	4
22	I know at least one teenage girl who has had an abortion.	1	2	3	4
23	Prostitution is a problem in my community.	1	2	3	4
24	I have been pressured by a partner to have sex.	1	2	3	4
25	I am currently growing up without a father.	1	2	3	4

	PLEASE CIRCLE ONLY ONE RESPONSE!	Strongly Disagree	Disagree	Agree	Strongly Agree
26	I have a male role model in my life whom I look up to.	1	2	3	4
27	I feel depressed most of the time.	1	2	3	4
28	At least one person who is close to me is suffering from mental illness.	1	2	3	4
29	At least one person who is close to me has been physically abused by his/her parents.	1	2	3	4
30	I feel that people hold negative stereotypes about my community.	1	2	3	4
31	I sometimes do things that I don't want to do because my friends pressure me to do them.	1	2	3	4
32	I feel comfortable leaving my neighborhood and going to other parts of Los Angeles.	1	2	3	4
33	I think that tagging is an art form.	1	2	3	4
34	Graffiti makes my community look ugly.	1	2	3	4
35	I often see stray animals in my community.	1	2	3	4
36	Please circle your grade level.	9	10	11	12
37	Please circle your gender.	Male		Female	
38	Please circle your race.	African American		Latino/a	Other

Genius Hour Project Description

As part of its business model, Google encourages its developers to spend 20% of their work time engaged in passion projects of their own choosing. The idea is that when creative people are given the opportunity to play and explore what interests them, they will develop innovative ideas and achieve a level of personal and professional fulfillment that ultimately will benefit everyone—the employees and the company.

This practice helped inspire the idea for Genius Hour, which is an educational model being used in classrooms across the country. If interest-driven learning, problem solving, and creativity work for Google, why can't they work for our public education system? Instead of always telling students what to do, why not see what happens when they direct their own learning?

We are going to adopt this model in our classroom. The only way that you will feel comfortable integrating new and multimodal literacies into your English instruction is if you have the chance to gain mastery of tools on your own first. And I'm not going to tell you which tools to choose—that's up to you.

You are going to choose a digital tool that you want to learn more about and conduct your own exploration into how it works, what you can do with it, and how it can be used in the English classroom. You should choose a tool that you are NOT FAMILIAR WITH—this should be a journey of discovery! You also should choose a tool that is NOT DIRECTLY EDUCATIONAL—I want you to make those connections.

You will give a 15-minute interactive presentation to your classmates that answers the following five questions:

1. What kind of learning curve did you have to navigate to start using this tool?
2. What did you find interesting as you explored what others have done with this tool?
3. What have you created with this tool?
4. What can you ask us to do with this tool during your presentation?
5. What can English teachers do with this tool?

For more information about Genius Hour, check out www.youtube.com/watch?v=NMFQUtHsWhc

ENGL 5342: New and Multimodal Literacies—Rubric: Genius Hour Presentation

	1 point	2 points	3 points	Your Score:
Digital Tool Analysis	Analysis of tool does not demonstrate understanding of major concepts/ideas of multimodality and the connections to teaching; misunderstanding or lack of evidence supporting claims.	Analysis of tool is superficial; may not explicitly identify and analyze major concepts and ideas of multimodality; superficial understanding of teaching connections; weak evidence to support claims.	Analysis of tool is comprehensive, noting major concepts and themes of multimodality and the connection those ideas have to teachers' work in the classroom with evidence supporting claims.	
Real-World Connections	Presentation explores the tool in isolation and makes no effort to connect themes to current educational or social issues.	Presentation makes vague or general attempt to relate tool to current issues facing schools, society, or popular culture.	Presentation makes explicit and thoughtful connections between the tool and current issues facing schools, society, or popular culture.	
Active Learning Strategies	Activities rely on direct transmission of information and engage few or no classmates.	Activities engage most classmates in active grappling with ideas from the text.	Activities engage all classmates in active learning, using a student-centered model of teaching.	
Presentation Materials	Presentation does not use engaging multimedia format AND does not provide classmates with information for their toolbox.	Presentation either does not use multimedia format OR does not provide classmates with information for their toolbox.	Presentation uses engaging format incorporating multimedia and is shared with classmates for their toolbox.	
Use of Course Readings	Ideas from course readings are not referenced during the presentation	Ideas from one course reading are referenced during the presentation	Ideas from AT LEAST three course readings are referenced during the presentation.	

Multiple Views on the Purpose of Literacy Instruction

TRADITIONAL APPROACHES TO LITERACY
(excerpted from Freire & Macedo, 1987)

Academic Approach

In this case, reading is viewed as the acquisition of predefined forms of knowledge and is organized around the study of Latin and Greek and the mastery of the great classic works. Since it would be unrealistic to expect the vast majority of society to meet such high standards, reading was redefined as the acquisition of reading skills, decoding skills, vocabulary development, and so on. This second rationale served to legitimize a dual approach to reading—one level for the ruling class and another for the dispossessed majority.

Utilitarian Approach

The major goal of this approach is to produce readers who meet the basic reading requirements of contemporary society. This position has led to the development of "functional literates," groomed primarily to meet the requirements of our ever more complex technological society. This notion of literacy has been enthusiastically incorporated as a major goal by the back-to-basics proponents of reading. It also has contributed to the development of neatly packaged reading programs that are presented as the solution to difficulties students experience in reading job application forms, tax forms, advertisement literature, sales catalogs, labels, and the like.

Cognitive Development Approach

The cognitive development model stresses the construction of meaning whereby readers engage in a dialectical interaction between themselves and the objective world. Although the acquisition of literacy skills is viewed as an important task in this approach, the salient feature is how people construct meaning through problem-solving processes. Comprehension of the text is relegated to a position of lesser importance in favor of the development of new cognitive structures that can enable students to move from simple to highly complex reading tasks.

Romantic Approach

Like the cognitive development model, the romantic approach is based on an interactionist approach with a major focus on the construction of meaning; however, the romantic approach views meaning as being generated by the reader and not occurring in the interaction between reader and author via text. The romantic approach greatly emphasizes the affective and sees reading as the fulfillment of self and a joyful experience. In essence, the romantic approach presents a counterpoint to the authoritarian modes of pedagogy, which view readers as "objects."

SOMETHING DIFFERENT: EMANCIPATORY APPROACH?

Emancipatory Literacy

Freire and Macedo: The new literacy programs must be based largely on the notion of emancipatory literacy, in which literacy is viewed as one of the major vehicles by which oppressed people are able to participate in the sociohistorical transformation of their society. In this view, literacy programs should be tied not only to mechanical learning of reading skills but, additionally, to a critical understanding of the overall goals for national reconstruction. Thus, the reader's development of a critical comprehension of the text, and the sociohistorical context to which it refers, becomes an important factor in our notion of literacy. The act of learning to read and write, in this instance, is a creative act that involves a critical comprehension of reality.

Literacy, in this sense, is grounded in a critical reflection on the cultural capital of the oppressed. It becomes a vehicle by which the oppressed are equipped with the necessary tools to re-appropriate their history, culture, and language practices.

Henry Giroux: Within this perspective, literacy is approached not merely as a technical skill to be acquired, but as a necessary foundation for cultural action for freedom. Literacy is inherently a political project in which men and women assert their right and responsibility not only to read, understand, and transform their own experiences, but also to reconstitute their relationship with the wider society. In this sense, literacy is fundamental to aggressively constructing one's voice as part of a wider project of possibility and empowerment.

Theresa Perry: The questions that are at the heart of the dilemma of schooling for African Americans, and perhaps for any group for whom there is not a predictable or rational relationship between effort and reward in the social, education, or economic spheres, are these: Why should you make an effort to excel in school if you cannot predict when and under what circumstances learning will be valued, seen, and acknowledged? Why should you focus on learning in school if that learning doesn't, in reality or in your imaginary community, have the capacity to affect, inform, or alter your self-perception or your status as a member of an oppressed group?

African Americans historically have given rich and elaborated answers to these questions. For African Americans, from slavery to the modern civil rights movement, the answers were these: You pursued learning because this is how you asserted yourself as a free person, how you claimed your humanity. You pursued learning so you could work for the racial uplift, for the liberation of your people. You pursued education so you could prepare yourself to lead your people.

References

Adichie, C. (2009). The danger of a single story. *TED Global Talk*. Retrieved from www.ted.com/talks/chimamanda_adichie_the_danger_of_a_single_story

Alexander, M. (2010). *The new Jim Crow: Mass incarceration in the age of colorblindness*. New York, NY: New Press.

American Association of School Librarians. (2012). *Filtering in schools: Impact of filtering on learning*. Chicago, IL: American Library Association.

American Political Science Association Task Force. (2004). American democracy in an age of rising inequality: Report of the American Political Science Association Task Force on Inequality and American Democracy. *Perspectives on Politics, 2*(4), 651–666.

Applebee, A. N., Langer, J. A., Nystrand, M., & Gamoran, A. (2003). Discussion-based approaches to developing understanding: Classroom instruction and student performance in middle and high school English. *American Educational Research Journal, 40*, 685–730.

Appleman, D. (2009). *Critical encounters in high school English: Teaching literary theory to adolescents* (2nd ed.). New York, NY: Teachers College Press.

Baker-Doyle, K. (2017). *Transformative teachers: Teacher leadership and learning in a connected world*. Cambridge, MA: Harvard University Press.

Bal, P. M., & Veltkamp, M. (2013). How does fiction reading influence empathy? An experimental investigation on the role of emotional transportation. *PLOS One, 8*(1).

Bartels, L. (2008). *Unequal democracy: The political economy of the new gilded age*. Princeton, NJ: Princeton University Press.

Barton, D., Hamilton, M., & Ivanic, R. (2000). *Situated literacies: Reading and writing in context*. New York, NY: Routledge.

Beach, R. (2005, November). *Conducting research on teaching literature: The influence of texts, contexts, and teacher responses to multicultural literature*. Paper presented at the National Reading Conference, Miami, FL.

Bennett, S., & Maton, K. (2010). Beyond the "digital natives" debate: Towards a more nuanced understanding of students' technology experiences. *Journal of Computer Assisted Learning, 26*(5), 321–331.

Bloom, H. (1994). *The Western canon: The books and school of the ages*. New York, NY: Riverhead Books.

Brown, C., & Czerniewicz, L. (2010). Debunking the "digital native": Beyond digital apartheid, towards digital democracy. *Journal of Computer Assisted Learning, 26*(5), 357–369.

Brown, W. (2015). *Undoing the demos: Neoliberalism's stealth revolution.* New York, NY: Zone Books.

Cammarota, J., & Fine, M. (2008). *Revolutionizing education: Youth participatory action research in motion.* New York, NY: Routledge.

Cazden, C. (2001). *Classroom discourse: The language of teaching and learning* (2nd ed.). New York, NY: Heinemann.

Centers for Disease Control and Prevention. (2013). CDC health disparities and inequalities report—United States, 2013. *MMWR, 62.*

Coiro, J., Knobel, M., Lankshear, C., & Lue, D. (Eds.). (2012). *Handbook of research on new literacies.* New York, NY: Routledge.

Cridland-Hughes, S. (2012). Literacy as social action in city debate. *Journal of Adolescent & Adult Literacy, 56*(3), 194–202.

de los Rios, C. (2017). Picturing ethnic studies: Photovoice and youth literacies of social action. *Journal of Adolescent & Adult Literacy, 61*(1), 15–24.

Delgado-Bernal, D. (1998). Using a Chicana feminist epistemology in educational research. *Harvard Educational Review, 68*(4), 555–582.

Desmond, M. (2016). *Evicted: Poverty and profit in the American city.* New York, NY: Crown.

Dewey, J. (1916). *Democracy and education: An introduction to the philosophy of education.* New York, NY: Macmillan.

DiFonzo, N. (2008). *The watercooler effect: An indispensable guide to understanding and harnessing the power of rumors.* New York, NY: Avery.

Duncan-Andrade, J., & Morrell, E. (2008). *The art of critical pedagogy: Possibilities for moving from theory to practice in urban schools.* New York, NY: Peter Lang.

Durlak, J., Weissberg, R., Dymnicki, A., Taylor, R., & Schellinger, K. (2011). The impact of enhancing students' social and emotional learning: A meta-analysis of school-based universal interventions. *Child Development, 82*(1), 405–432.

Erikson, E. H. (1968). *Identity: Youth and crisis.* New York, NY: Norton.

Faggella-Luby, M., Ware, S., & Capozzoli, A. (2009). Adolescent literacy—Reviewing adolescent literacy reports: Key components and critical questions. *Journal of Literacy Research, 41*, 453–475.

Fang, Z. (1996). A review of research on teacher beliefs and practices. *Educational Research, 38*(1), 47–65.

Freire, P. (1970). *Pedagogy of the oppressed.* New York, NY: Bloomsbury Press.

Freire, P. (2007). *Teachers as cultural workers: Letters to those who dare teach.* New York, NY: Routledge.

Freire, P., & Macedo, D. (1987). *Literacy: Reading the word and the world.* Westport, CT: Bergin & Garvey.

Gagnon, P. (2003). *Educating democracy: State standards to ensure a civic core.* Washington, DC: Albert Shanker Institute.

Garcia, A. (Ed.). (2014). *Teaching in the connected learning classroom.* Irvine, CA: Digital Media and Learning Research Hub.

Gray, L., Thomas, N., Lewis, L., & Tice, P. (2010). *Teachers' use of educational technology in U.S. public schools: 2009.* Washington, DC: National Center for Education Statistics.

Greene, M. (2000). *Releasing the imagination: Essays on education, the arts, and social change.* San Francisco, CA: Jossey-Bass.

Griffin, P., McGaw, B., & Care, E. (Eds.). (2011). *Assessment and teaching of 21st century skills.* New York, NY: Springer.

Guillory, J. (1993). *Cultural capital: The problem of literary canon formation.* Chicago, IL: University of Chicago Press.

Gutierrez, K. D. (2008). Developing a sociocritical literacy in the third space. *Reading Research Quarterly, 43*(2), 148–164.

Harvey, D. (2007). Neoliberalism as creative destruction. *The ANNALS of the American Academy of Political and Social Science, 610,* 21–44.

Heirman, W., & Walrave, M. (2008). Assessing concerns and issues about the mediation of technology in cyberbullying. *Cyberpsychology: Journal of Psychosocial Research on Cyberspace, 2*(2), article 1.

Hess, D., & McAvoy, P. (2014). *The political classroom: Evidence and ethics in democratic education.* New York, NY: Routledge.

hooks, b. (1994). *Teaching to transgress: Education as the practice of freedom.* New York, NY: Routledge.

Horkheimer, M., & Adorno, T. (1947). *The dialectic of enlightenment.* New York, NY: Continuum.

Houston Independent School District. (2012). Houston Urban Debate League: Findings related to student performance, 2010–2011. Department of Research and Accountability. Retrieved from www.houstonisd.org/cms/lib2/TX01001591/Centricity/Domain/8269/PE_FederalTitlePrograms/HUDL%201011%20Report%20071012.pdf

Howard, J. (1963, May 24). Telling talk from a Negro writer. *Life, 54*(21).

International Reading Association & National Council of Teachers of English. (1996). *Standards for the English language arts.* Newark, DE: International Reading Association.

Ito, M., Gutierrez, K., Livingstone, S., Penuel, B., Rhodes, J., Salen, K., ... Watkins, S. C. (2013). *Connected learning: An agenda for research and design.* Irvine, CA: Digital Media and Learning Research Hub.

Janks, H. (2012). The importance of critical literacy. *English Teaching: Practice and Critique, 11*(1), 150–163.

Jenkins, H. (2013). *Spreadable media: Creating value and meaning in a networked culture.* New York, NY: New York University Press.

Jones, L., Newman, L., & Isay, D. (1998). *Our America: Life and death on the south side of Chicago.* New York, NY: Scribner.

Journell, W. (2016). Teacher political disclosure as parrhesia. *Teachers College Record, 118,* 1–36.

Justice, B., & Stanley, J. (2016). Teaching in the time of Trump. *Social Education, 80*(1), 36–41.

Kellner, D., & Share, J. (2007). Critical media literacy is not an option. *Learning Inquiry, 1,* 59–69.

Kelly, L. (2013). Hip-hop literature: The politics, poetics, and power of hip-hop in the English classroom. *English Journal, 102*(5), 51–56.

Kidd, D., & Castano, E. (2013). Reading literary fiction improves theory of mind. *Science, 342*(6156), 377–380.

Konrath, S., O'Brien, H., & Hsing, C. (2011). Changes in dispositional empathy in American college students over time: A meta-analysis. *Personality and Social Psychology Review, 15*(2), 180–198.

Lamott, A. (1995). *Bird by bird: Some instructions on writing and life.* New York, NY: Anchor Books.

Lankshear, C., & Knobel, M. (2003). *New literacies: Changing knowledge and classroom learning.* Buckingham, UK: Open University Press.

Lawy, R., & Biesta, G. (2007). Citizenship-as-practice: The educational implications of an inclusive and relational understanding of citizenship. *British Journal of Educational Studies, 54*(1), 34–50.

Lingard, B., Hayes, D., & Mills, M. (2003). Teachers and productive pedagogies: Contextualising, conceptualising, utilising. *Pedagogy, Culture and Society, 11*(3), 397–422.

Lipman, P. (2011). *The new political economy of urban education: Neoliberalism, race, and the right to the city.* New York, NY: Routledge.

Lytle, S. L., Portnoy, D., Waff, D., & Buckley, M. (2009). Teacher research in urban Philadelphia: Twenty years working within, against, and beyond the system. *Educational Action Research, 17*(1), 23–42.

Mar, R., & Oatley, K. (2008). The function of fiction is the abstraction and simulation of social experience. *Perspectives on Psychological Science, 3*(3), 173–192.

Martinez, D. (2017). Imagining a language of solidarity for Black and Latinx youth in English language arts classrooms. *English Education, 49*(2), 179–196.

McLaren, P., & Kincheloe, J. (2007). *Critical pedagogy: Where are we now?* New York, NY: Peter Lang.

Minneapolis Public Schools. (2015). 2014–2015 Urban Debate League MPS evaluation. Research, evaluation and assessment: Minneapolis Public Schools. Retrieved from http://urbandebate.org/Why-It-Matters

Mirra, N., Garcia, A., & Morrell, E. (2015). *Doing youth participatory action research: Transforming inquiry with researchers, educators, and students.* New York, NY: Routledge.

Mirra, N., Honoroff, B., Elgendy, S., & Pietrzak, G. (2016). Reading and writing with a public purpose: Fostering middle school students' academic and critical community literacies through debate. *Journal of Language and Literacy Education, 12*(1), 3–22.

Moll, L., Amanti, C., Neff, D., & Gonzalez, N. (1992). Funds of knowledge for teaching: Using a qualitative approach to connect homes and classrooms. *Theory into Practice 31*(2), 132–141.

Morrell, E. (2008). *Critical literacy and urban youth: Pedagogies of access, dissent and liberation.* New York, NY: Routledge.

Morrison, T. (1992). *Playing in the dark: Whiteness and the literary imagination.* New York, NY: Vintage Books.

National Governors Association. (2010). Common Core State Standards for English language arts & literacy in history/social studies, science, and technical subjects. Washington, DC: Author.

New London Group. (1996). A pedagogy of multiliteracies: Designing social futures. *Harvard Educational Review, 66*(1), 60–92.

Nieto, S. (2006). *Teaching as political work: Learning from courageous and caring teachers.* The Longfellow Lecture. Child Development Institute: Sarah Lawrence College.

Nussbaum, M. (1997). *Poetic justice: The literary imagination and public life.* New York, NY: Beacon Press.

Oakes, J. (1992). Can tracking research inform practice? *Educational Researcher, 21*(4), 12–21.

Oatley, K. (2016). Fiction: Simulation of social worlds. *Trends in Cognitive Sciences, 20*(8), 618–628.

Obama, B. (2006). Obama to graduates: Cultivate empathy. Northwestern University News Center. Evanston, IL. Retrieved from www.northwestern.edu/newscenter/stories/2006/06/barack.html

O'Brien, D. G., Stewart, R. A., & Moje, E. B. (1995). Why content literacy is difficult to infuse into the secondary curriculum: Strategies, goals, and classroom realities. *Reading Research Quarterly, 30*, 442–463.

Pajares, M. F. (1992). Teachers' beliefs and educational research: Cleaning up a messy construct. *Review of Educational Research, 62*(3), 307–332.

Paris, D., & Alim, H. S. (2017). *Culturally sustaining pedagogies: Teaching and learning for justice in a changing world.* New York, NY: Teachers College Press.

Partnership for 21st Century Learning. (2016). *Framework for 21st century learning.* Retrieved from www.p21.org/storage/documents/docs/P21_framework_0816.pdf

Pew Research Center. (2014). *Political polarization in the American public.* Retrieved from www.people-press.org/2014/06/12/political-polarization-in-the-american-public/

Pew Research Center. (2017). *The partisan divide on political values grows even wider.* Retrieved from http://www.people-press.org/2017/10/05/the-partisan-divide-on-political-values-grows-even-wider/

Phi Delta Kappan. (2016). Why school? The 48th annual PDK poll of the public's attitudes toward the public schools. *Phi Delta Kappan, 98*(1), 1–32.

Prensky, M. (2001). Digital natives, digital immigrants part 1. *On the Horizon, 9*(5), 1–6.

Prinz, J. (2014). Is empathy necessary for morality? In A. Coplan & P. Goldie (Eds.), *Empathy: Philosophical and psychological perspectives* (pp. 211–229). New York, NY: Oxford University Press.

Purcell, K., Heaps, A., Buchanan, J., & Friedrich, L. (2013). *How teachers are using technology at home and in their classrooms.* Washington, DC: Pew Research Center's Internet and American Life Project.

Raymond, A. (1997). Inconsistency between a beginning elementary school teacher's mathematics beliefs and teaching practice. *Journal for Research in Mathematics Education, 28*(5), 550–576.

Ribble, M. (2015). *Digital citizenship in school* (3rd ed.). Arlington, VA: International Society for Technology in Education.

Rogers, J., Franke, M., Yun, J. E., Ishimoto, M., Diera, C., Geller, R., . . . & Brenes, T. (2017). *Teaching and learning in the age of Trump: Increasing stress and hostility in America's high schools.* Los Angeles, CA: UCLA's Institute for Democracy, Education, and Access.

Rogers, J., & Westheimer, J. (2017). Teaching about economic inequality in a diverse democracy: Politics, ideology, and difference. *PS: Political Science and Politics, 50*(4), 1049–1055.

Snow, C., Lawrence, J., & White, C. (2009). Generating knowledge of academic language among urban middle school students. *Journal of Research on Educational Effectiveness, 2*(4), 325–344.

Torney-Purta, J., & Vermeer, S. (2004). *Developing citizenship competencies from kindergarten through grade 12: A background paper for policymakers and educators.* Denver, CO: Education Commission of the States.

Turkle, S. (2012). *Alone together: Why we expect more from technology and less from each other.* New York, NY: Basic Books.

Tyack, D., & Cuban, L. (1995). *Tinkering toward utopia: A century of public school reform.* Cambridge, MA: Harvard University Press.

Warren, C. (2015). Conflicts and contradictions: Conceptions of empathy and the work of good-intentioned early career white female teachers. *Urban Education, 50*(5), 572–600.

Watts, R., & Flanagan, C. (2007). Pushing the envelope on civic engagement: A developmental and liberation psychology perspective. *The Journal of Community Psychology, 35,* 779–792.

Westheimer, J., & Kahne, J. (2004). What kind of citizen? The politics of educating for democracy. *American Educational Research Journal, 41*(2), 237–269.

Wilhelm, J. (2008). *"You gotta be the book": Teaching engaged and reflective reading with adolescents.* New York, NY: Teachers College Press.

Williams, W. C. (1955). *Journey to love.* New York, NY: Random House.

Yosso, T. (2006). *Critical race counterstories along the Chicana/Chicano educational pipeline.* New York, NY: Routledge.

Youniss, J., McLellan, J., & Yates, M. (1997). What we know about engendering civic identity. *American Behavioral Scientist, 40*(5), 620–631.

Zunshine, L. (2006). *Why we read fiction: Theory of mind and the novel.* Athens, OH: Ohio University Press.

Index

About the Author

Nicole Mirra is an assistant professor of urban teacher education in the Graduate School of Education at Rutgers University. She previously taught high school English and debate in New York City and Los Angeles public schools. Her research explores the intersections of critical literacy and civic engagement with youth and teachers across classroom, community, and digital learning environments. Central to her research and teaching agenda is a commitment to honoring and amplifying the literacy practices and linguistic resources that students from minoritized communities bring to civic life. Her work has appeared in *Review of Research in Education, Journal of Literacy Research, International Journal of Qualitative Studies in Education, Urban Education,* and more. She is a coauthor of *Doing Youth Participatory Action Research: Transforming Inquiry with Researchers, Educators, and Students* (Routledge, 2015).